Kinder Malen eingestellt
Raum, Haie, Sport und mehr

Coloring Pages for Kids

Coloring Pages for Kids
An imprint of Ciparum LLC

Kinder Malen eingestellt Raum, Haie, Sport und mehr
© 2017 Ciparum LLC
All rights reserved.
ISBN-10:1-63589-495-6
ISBN-13:978-1-63589-495-0

Coloring Pages for Kids

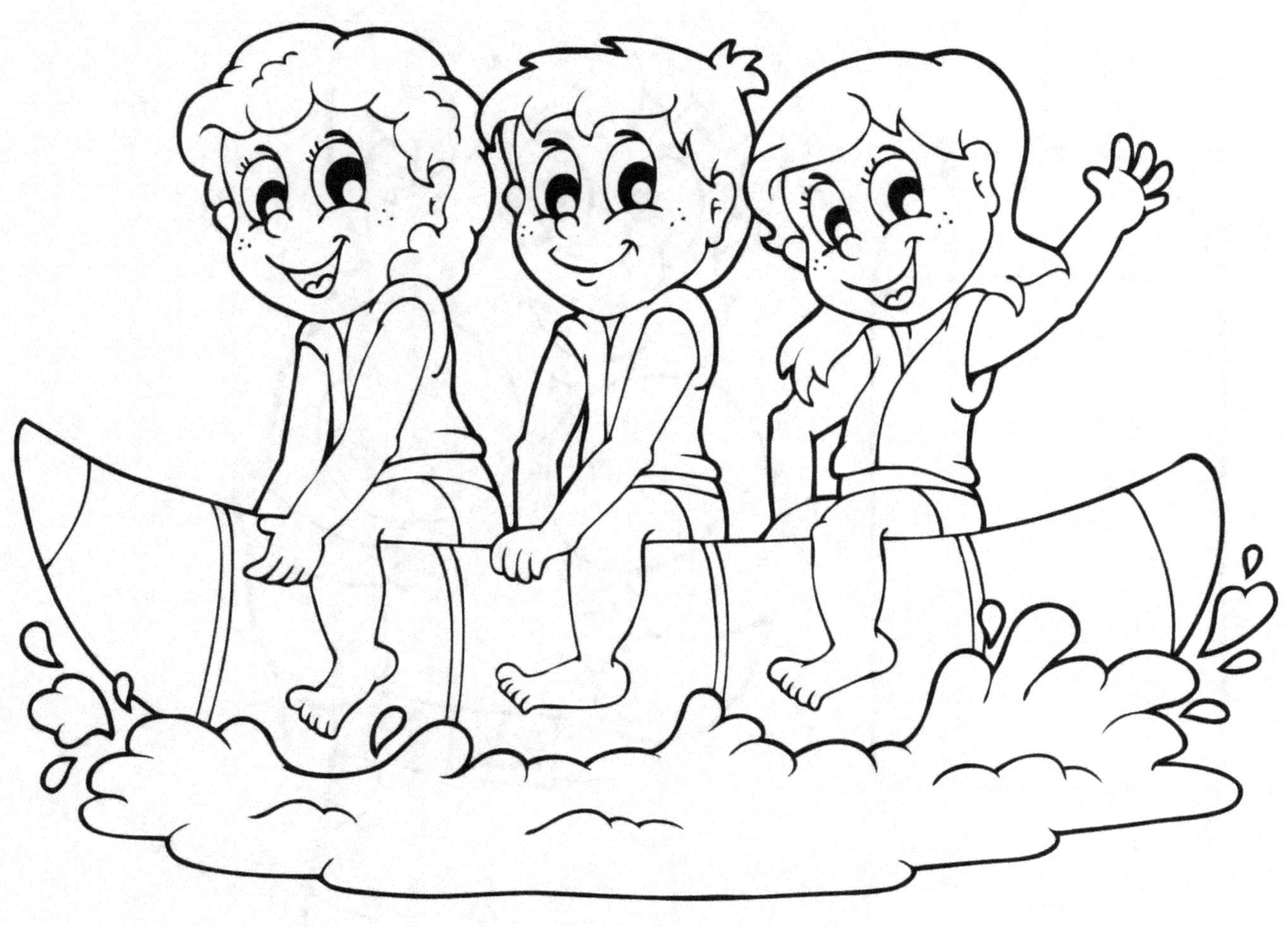

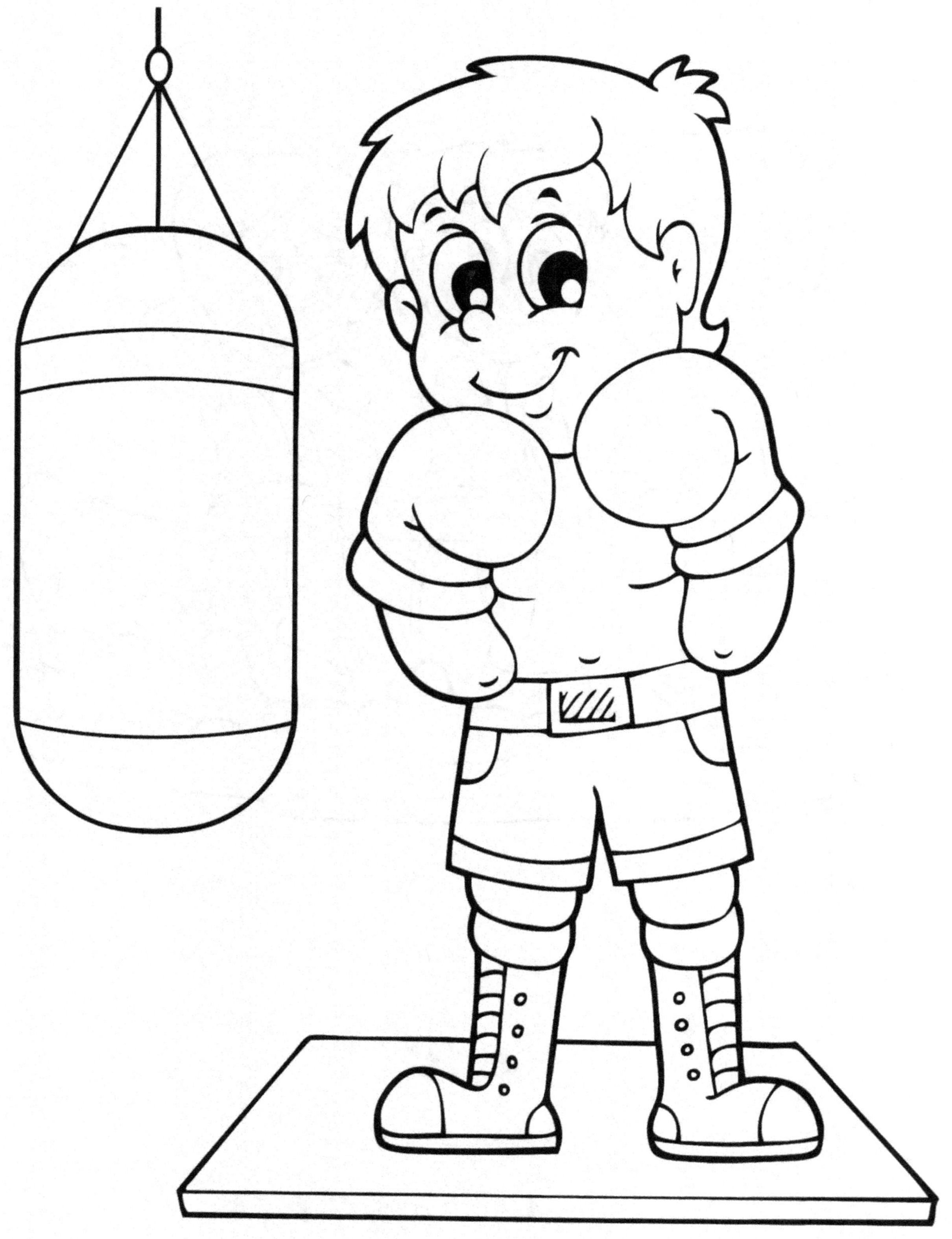

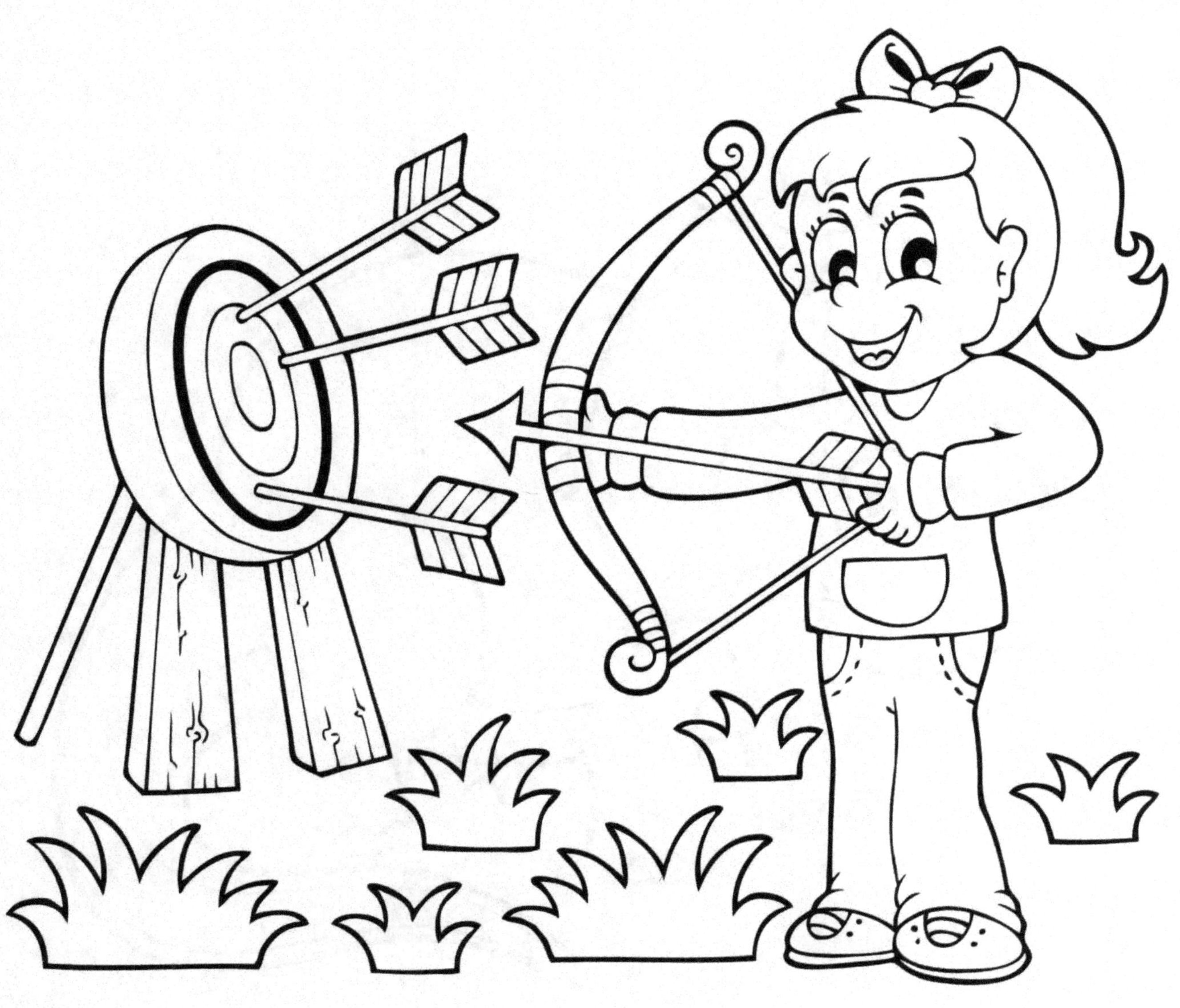

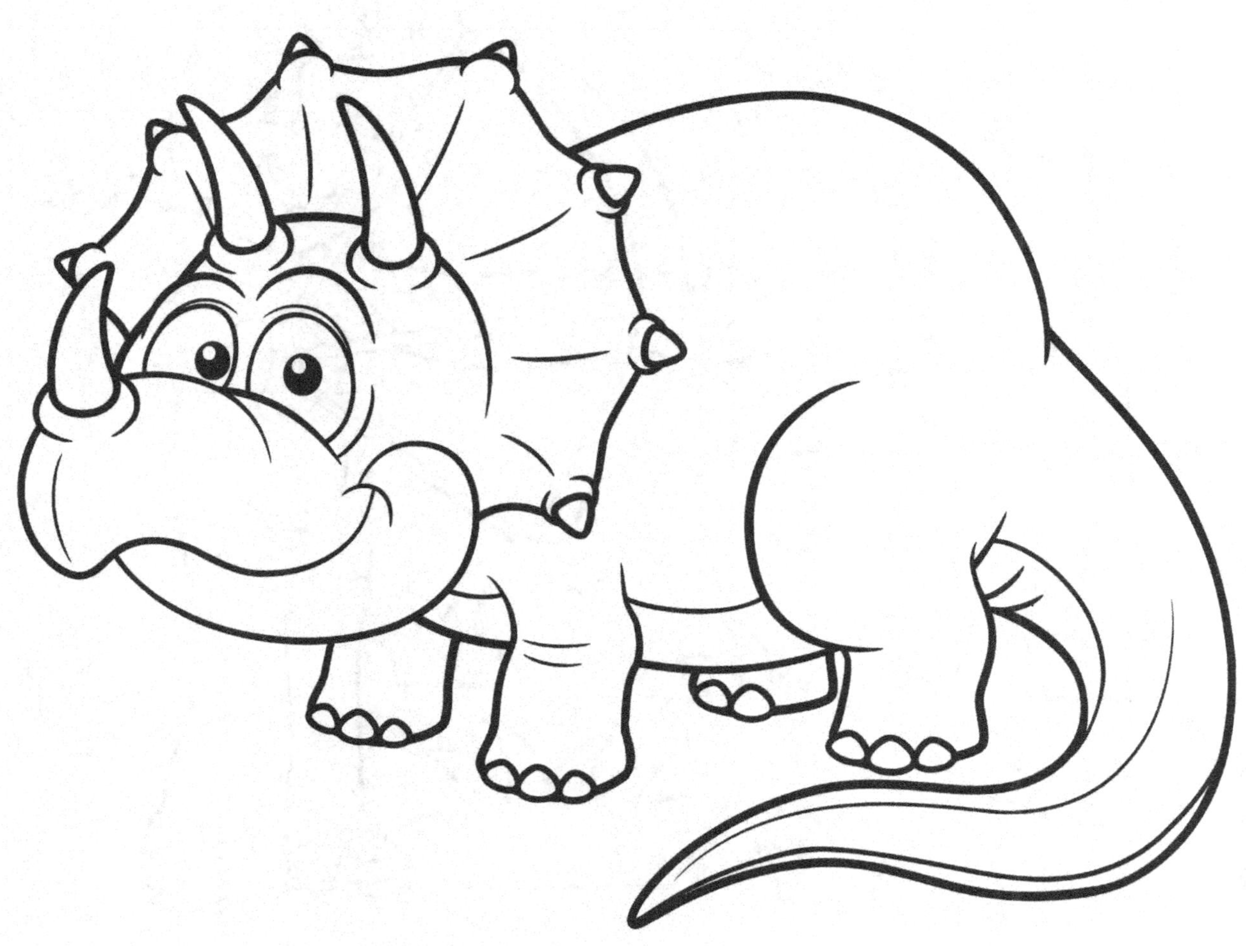

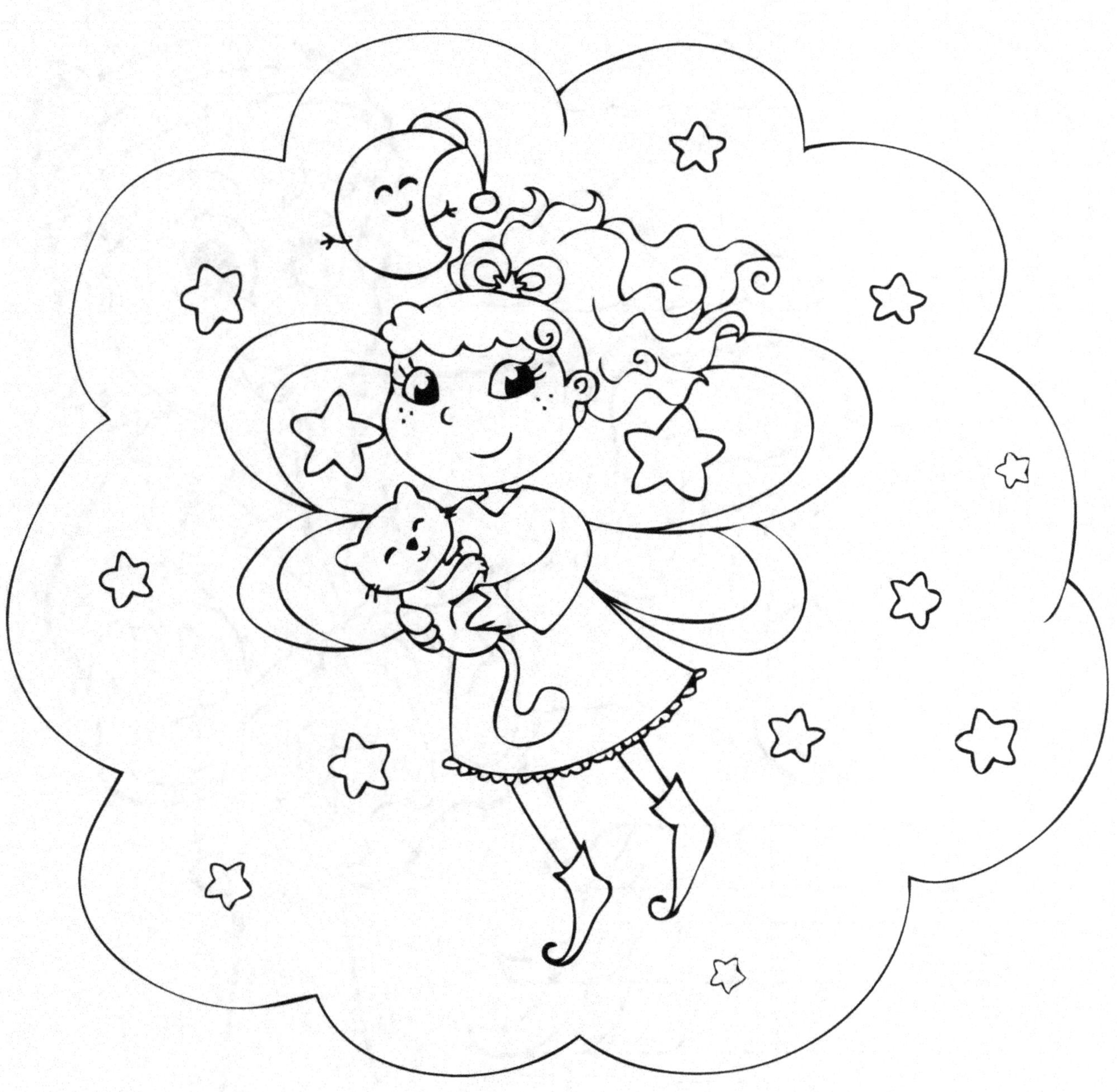

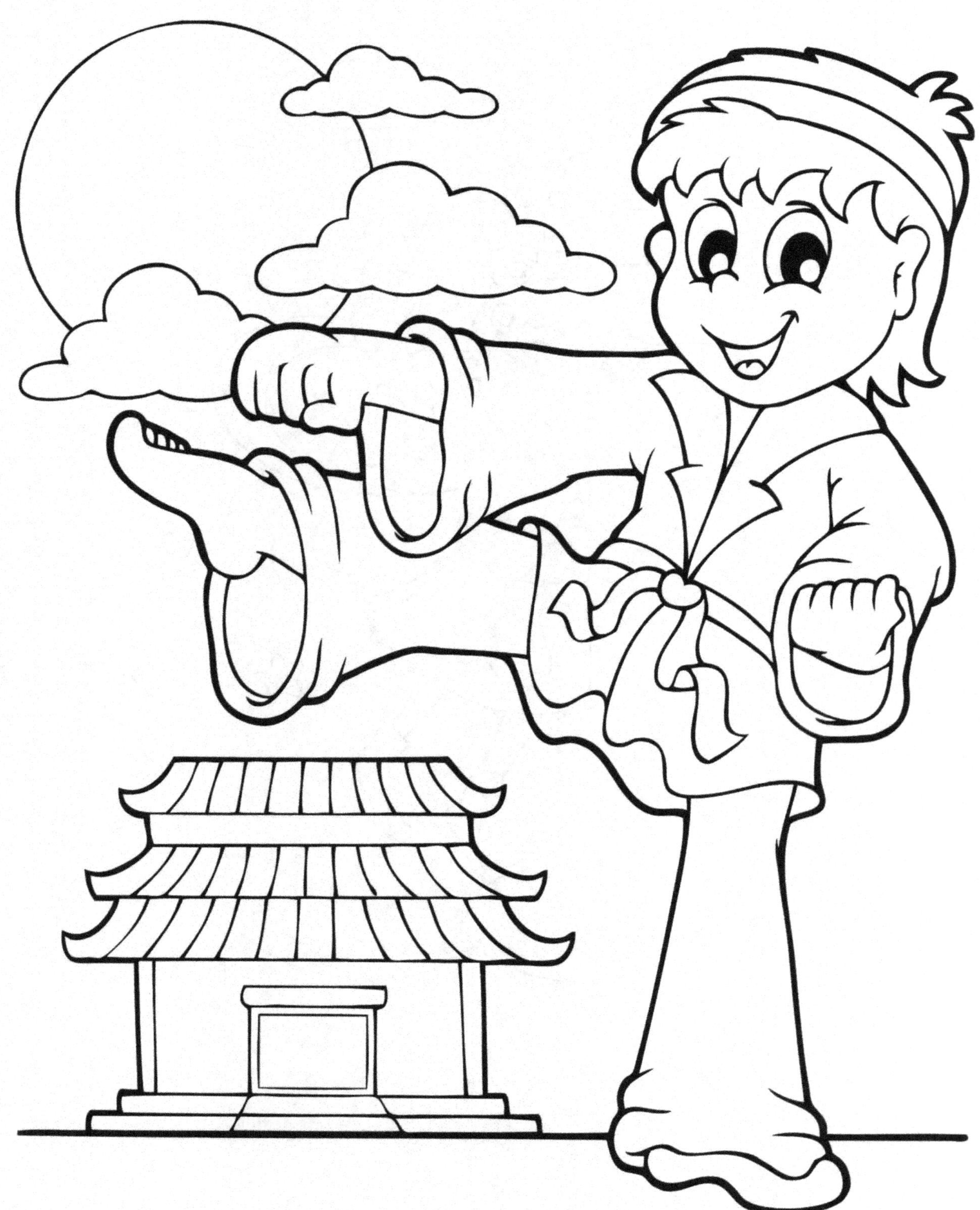

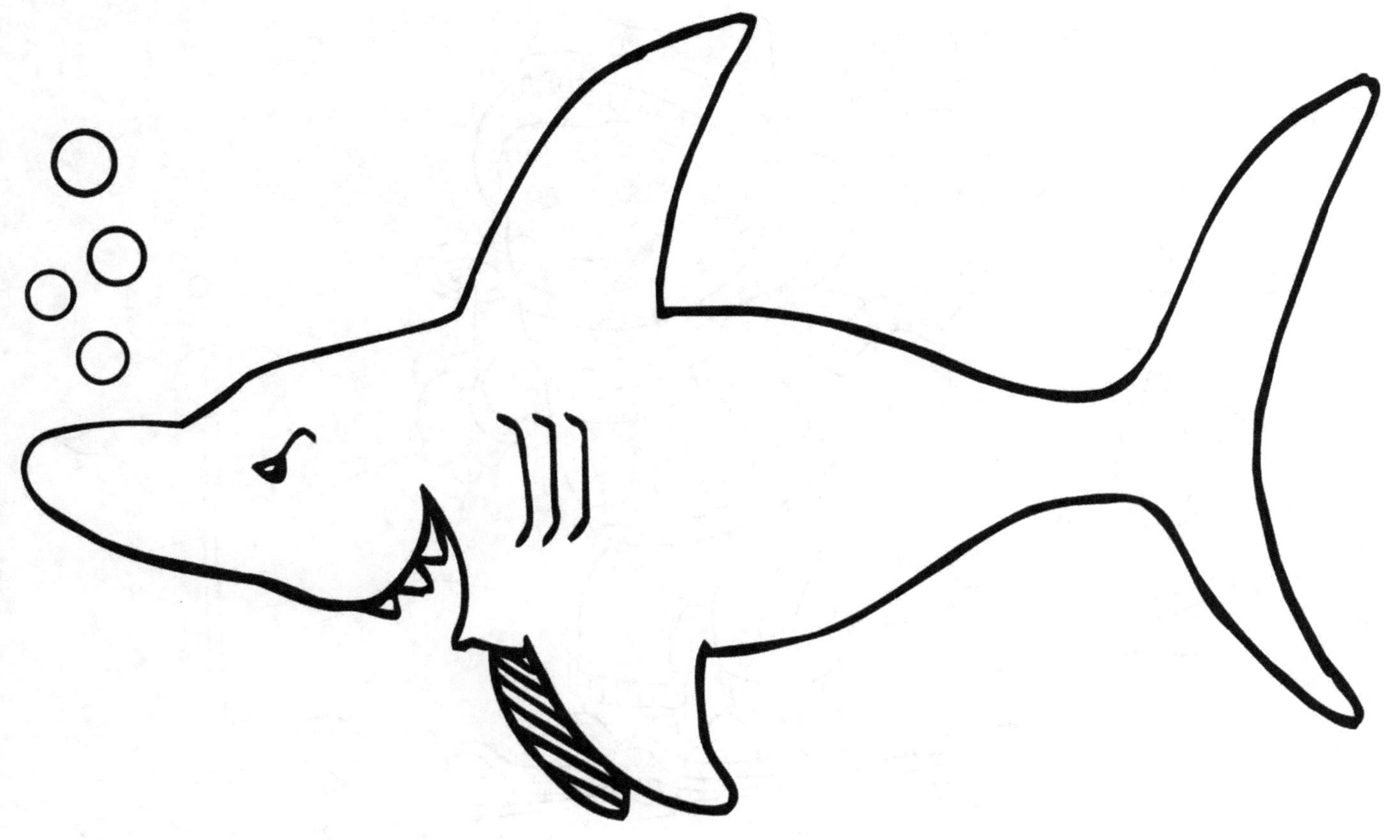

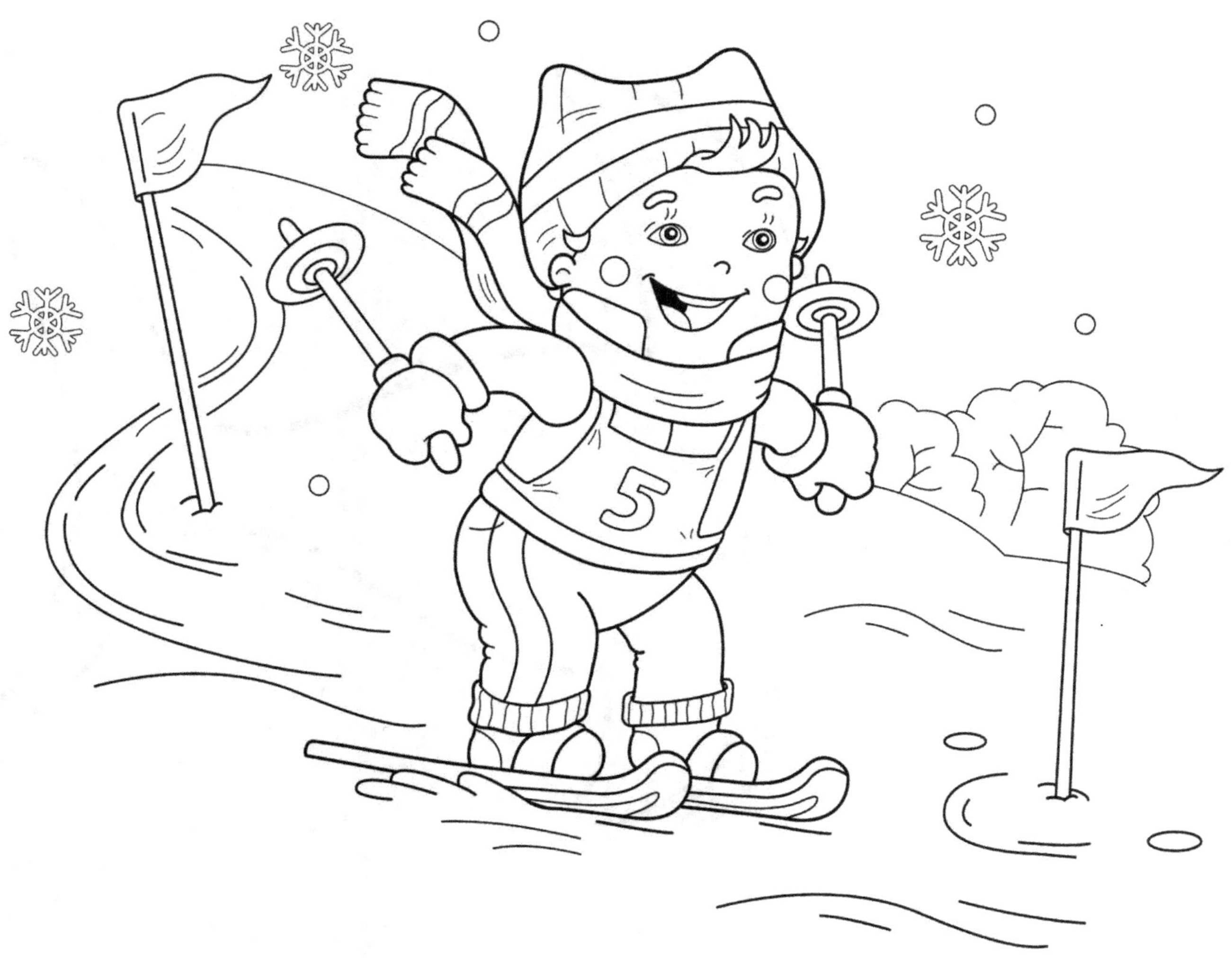

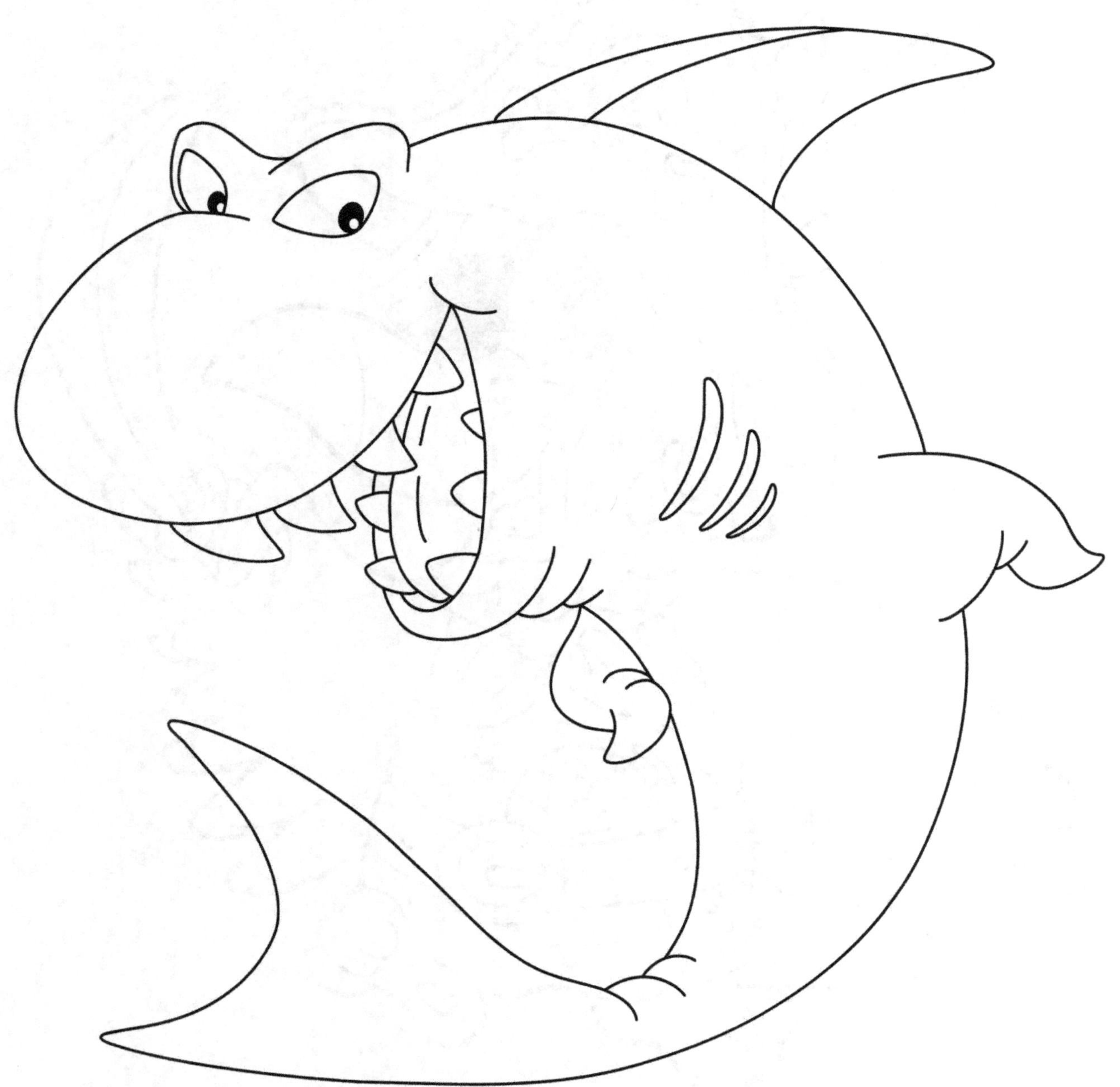

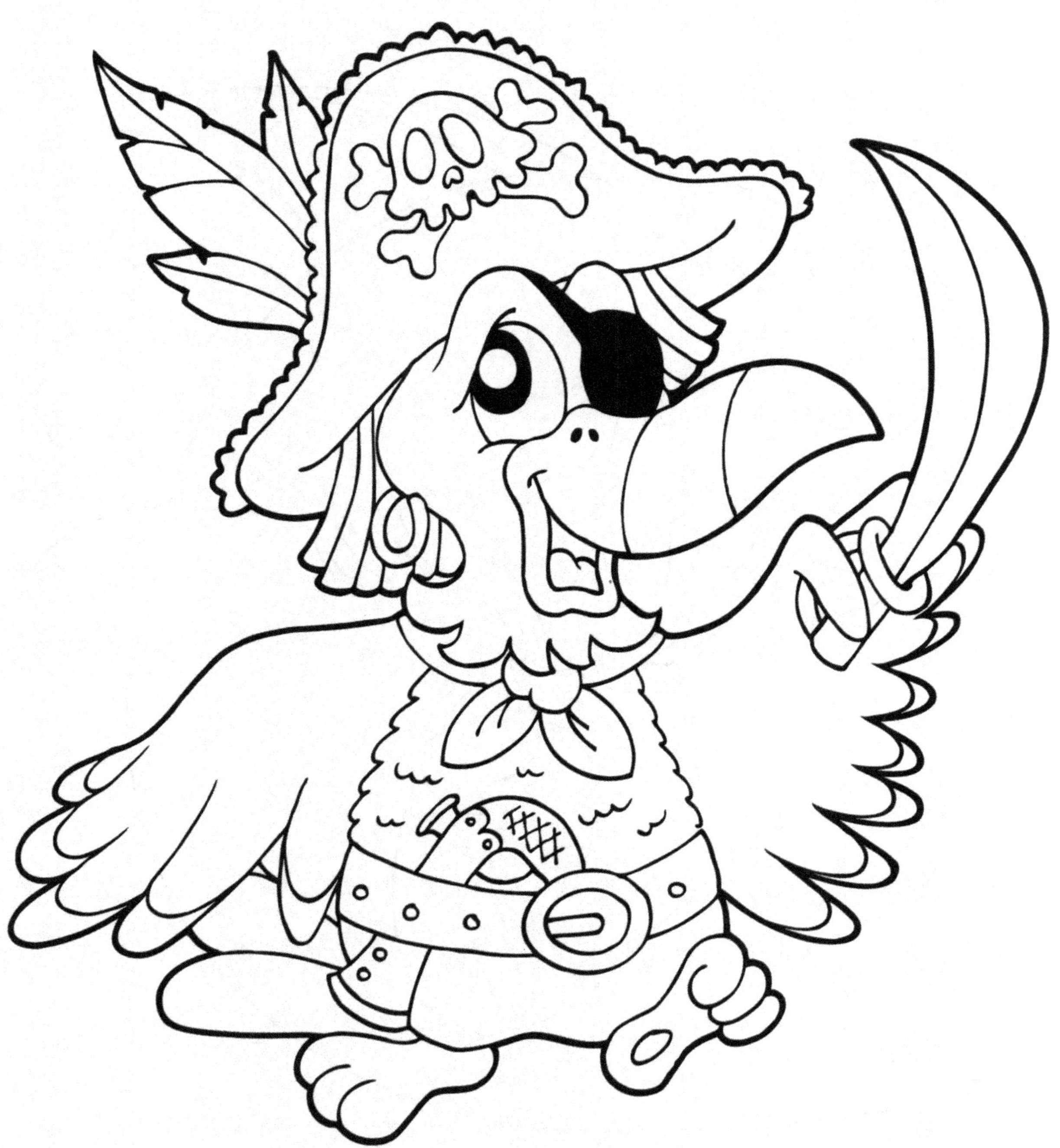

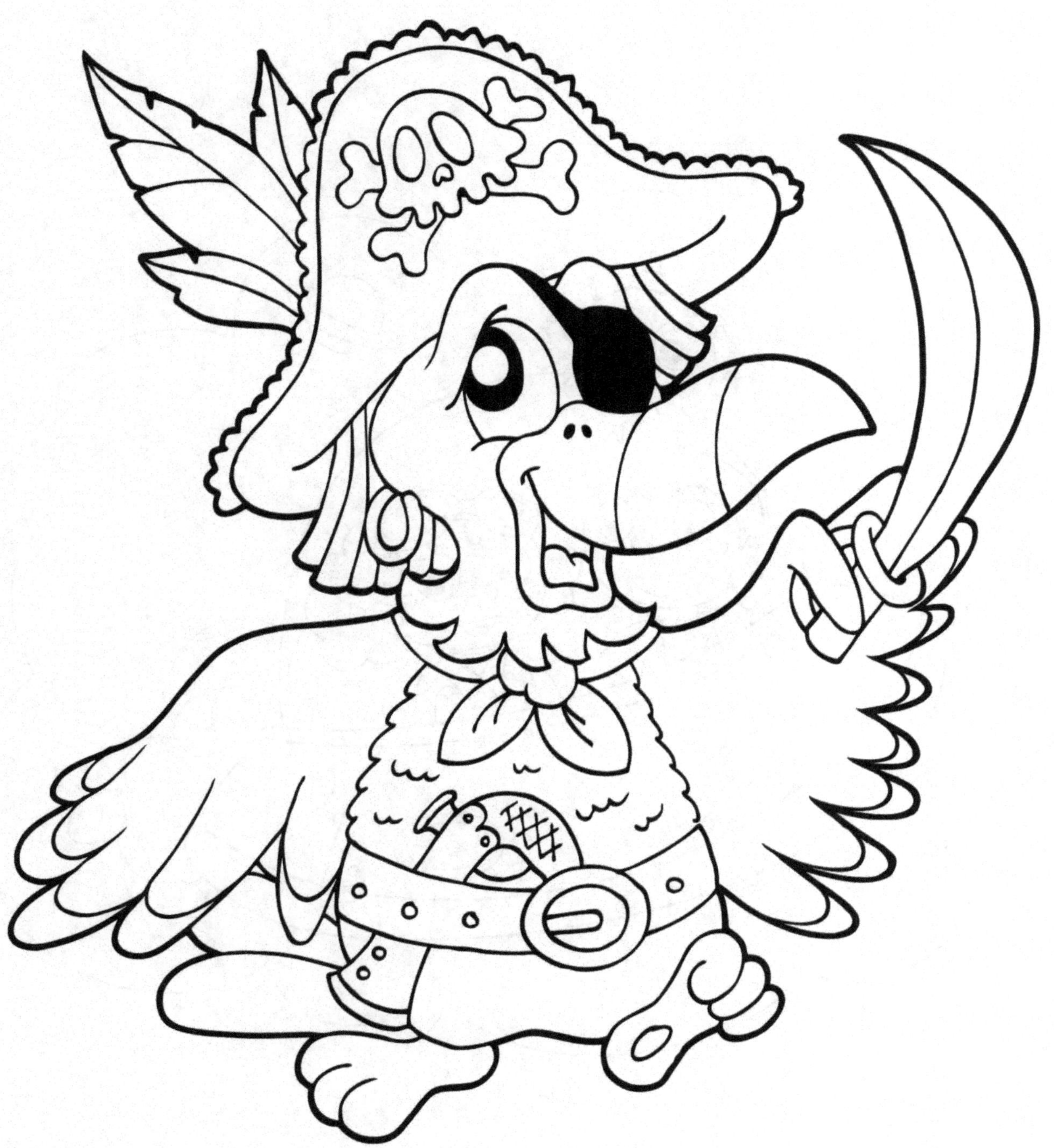

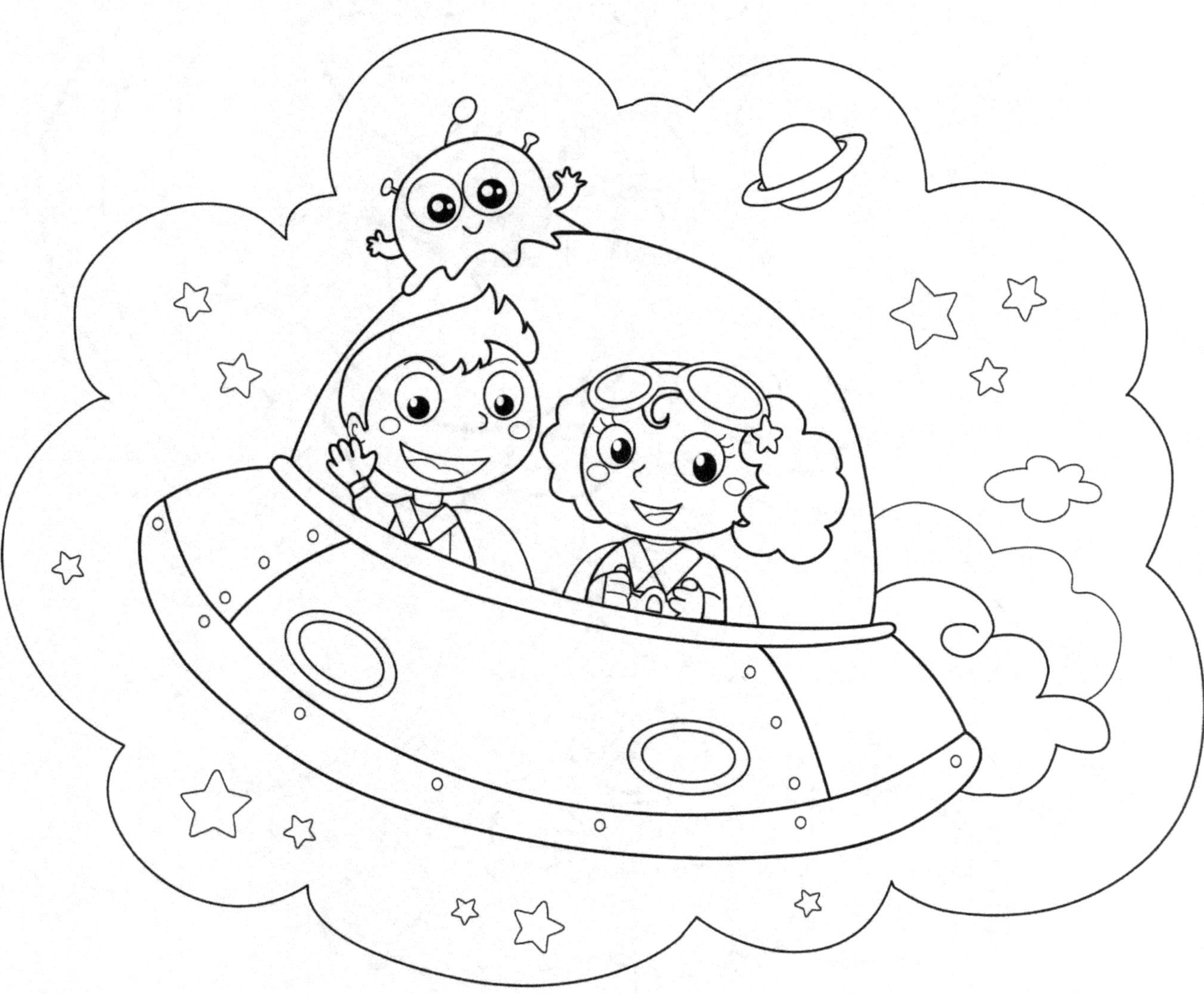

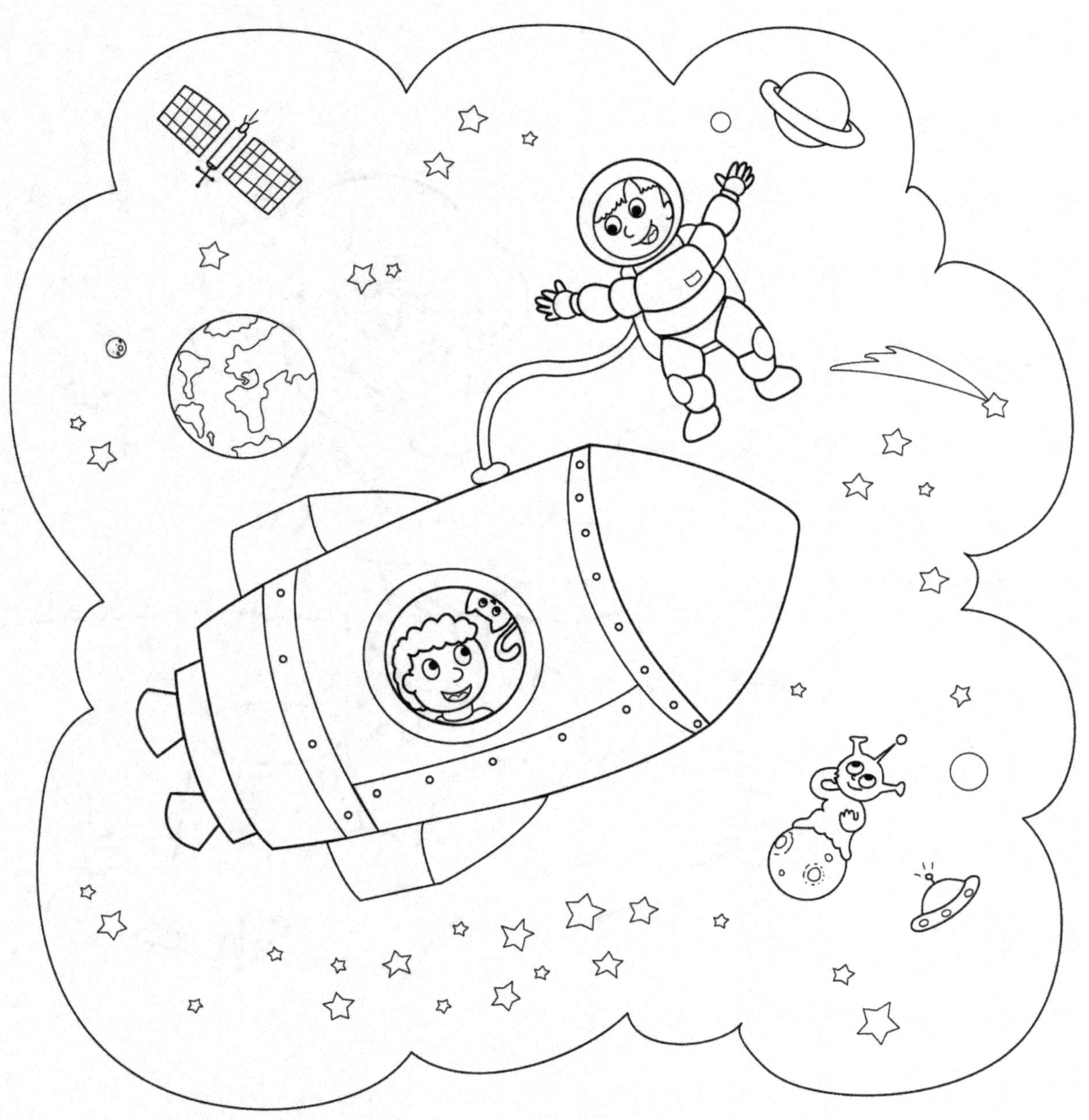

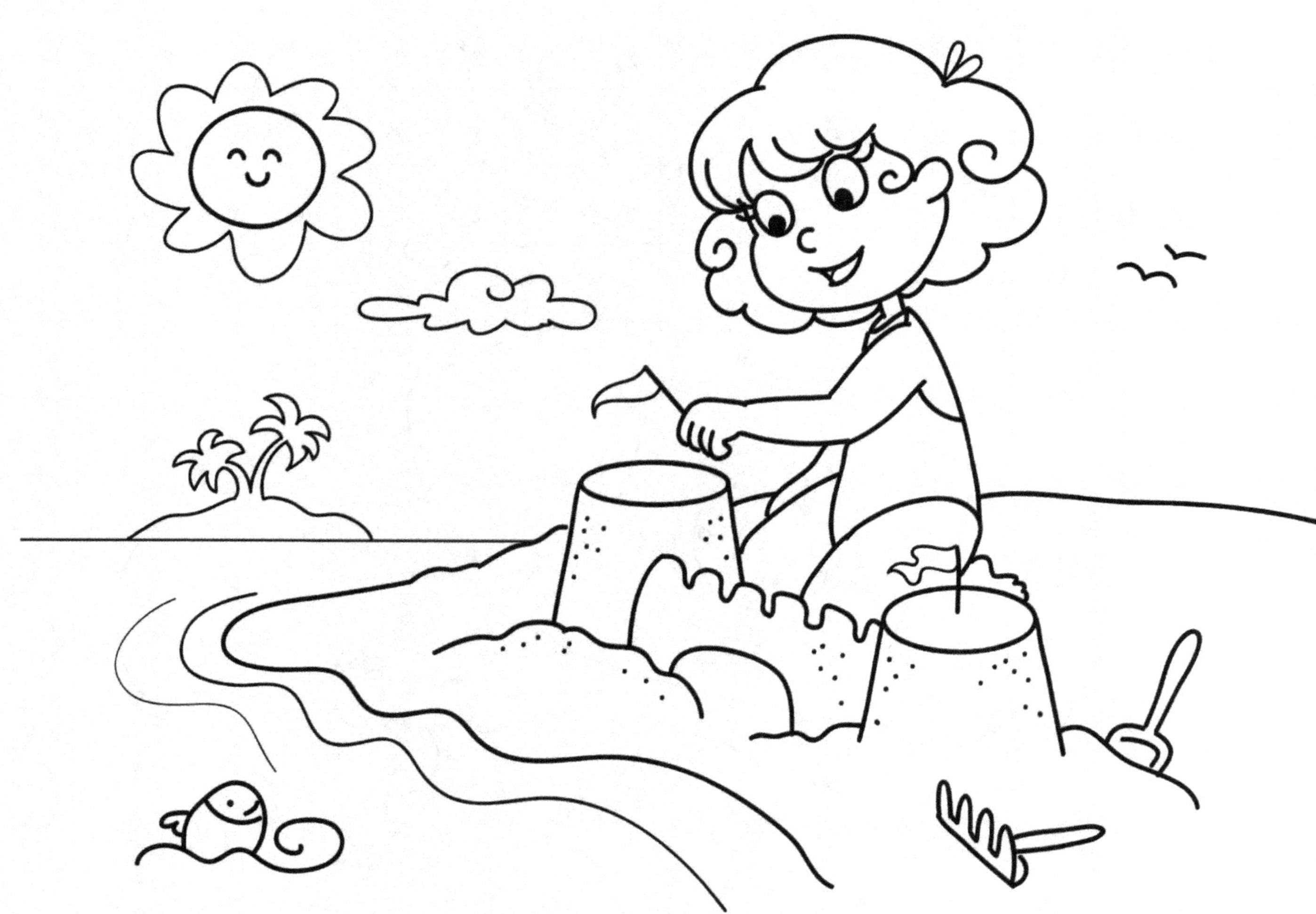

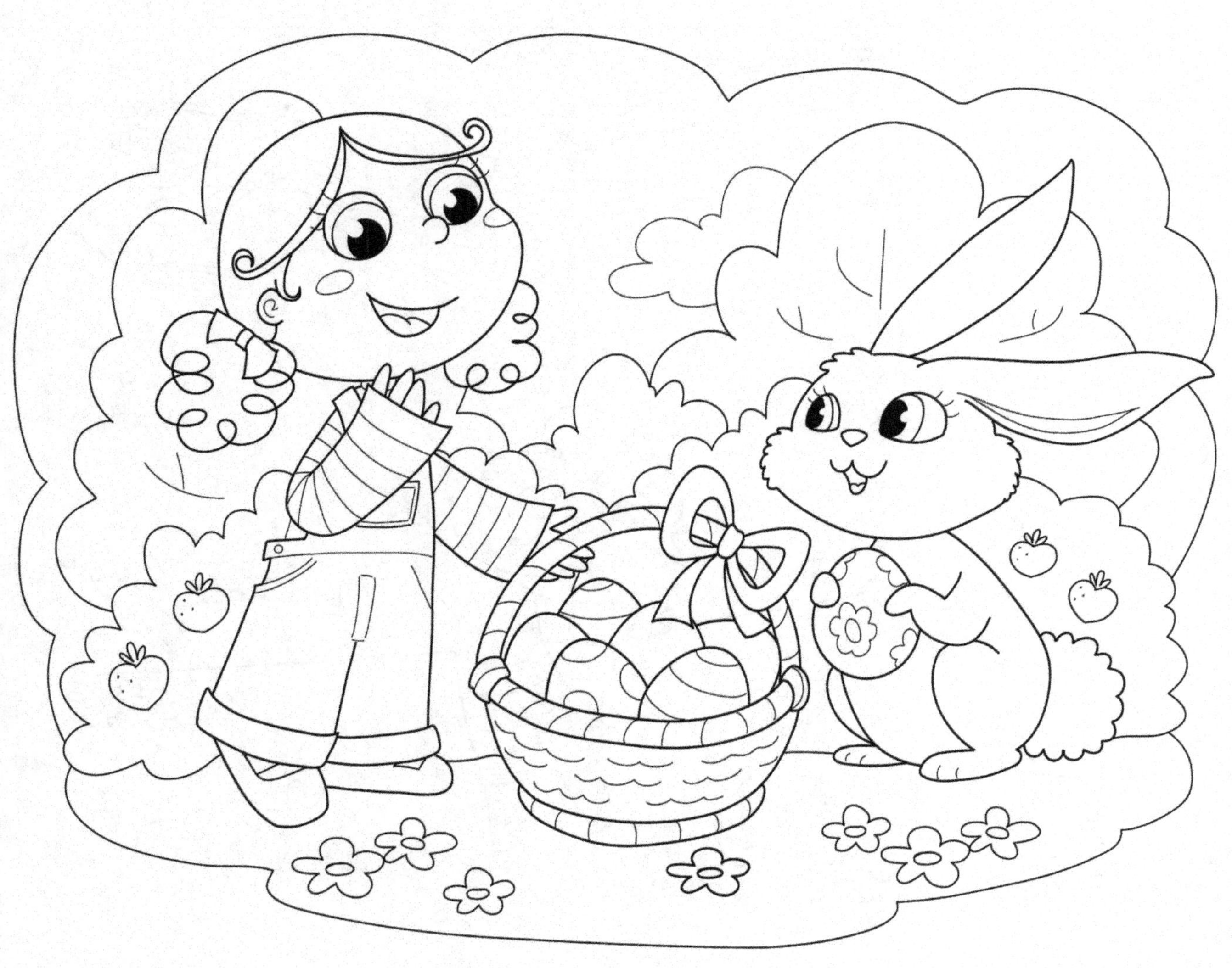

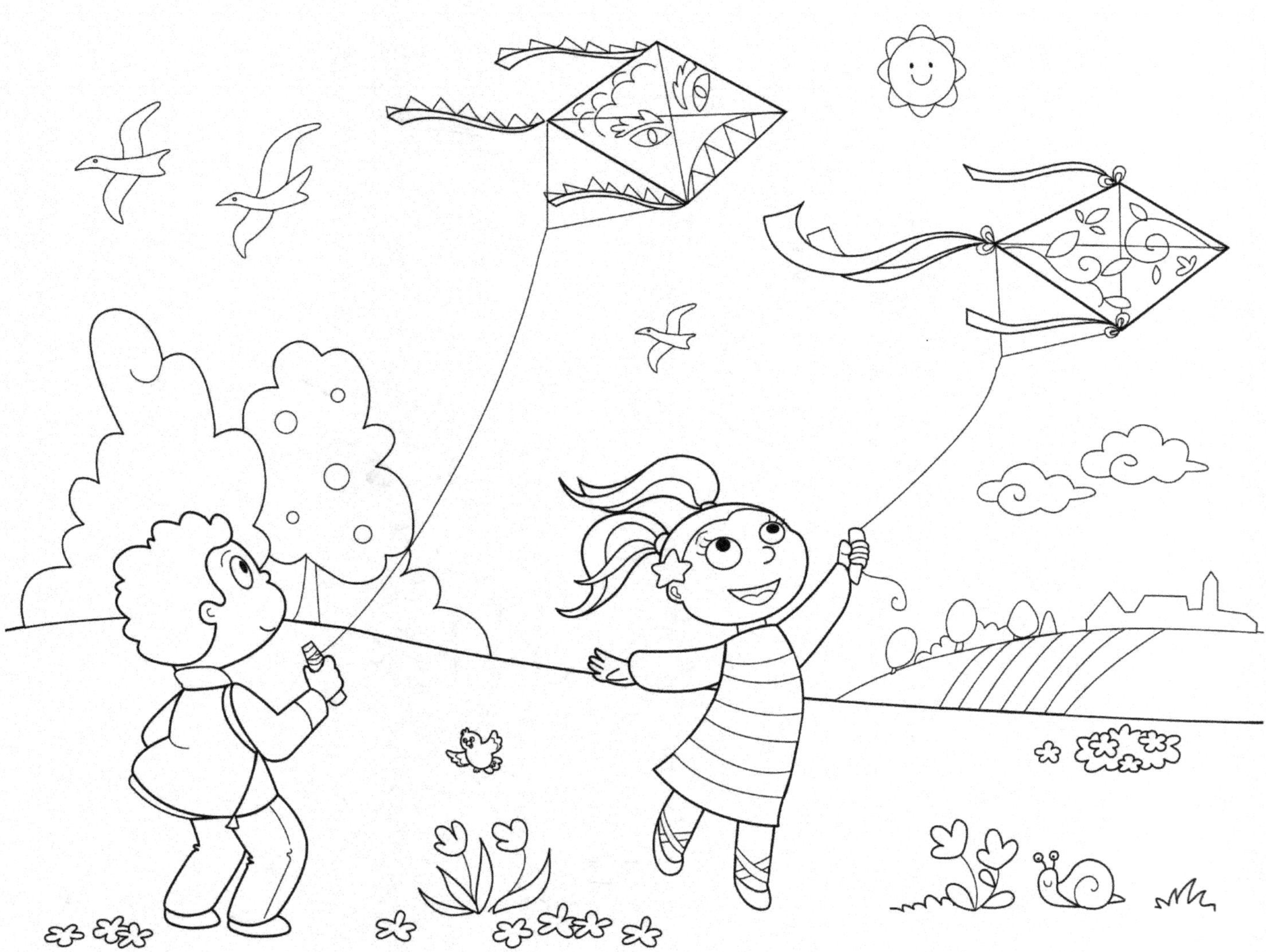

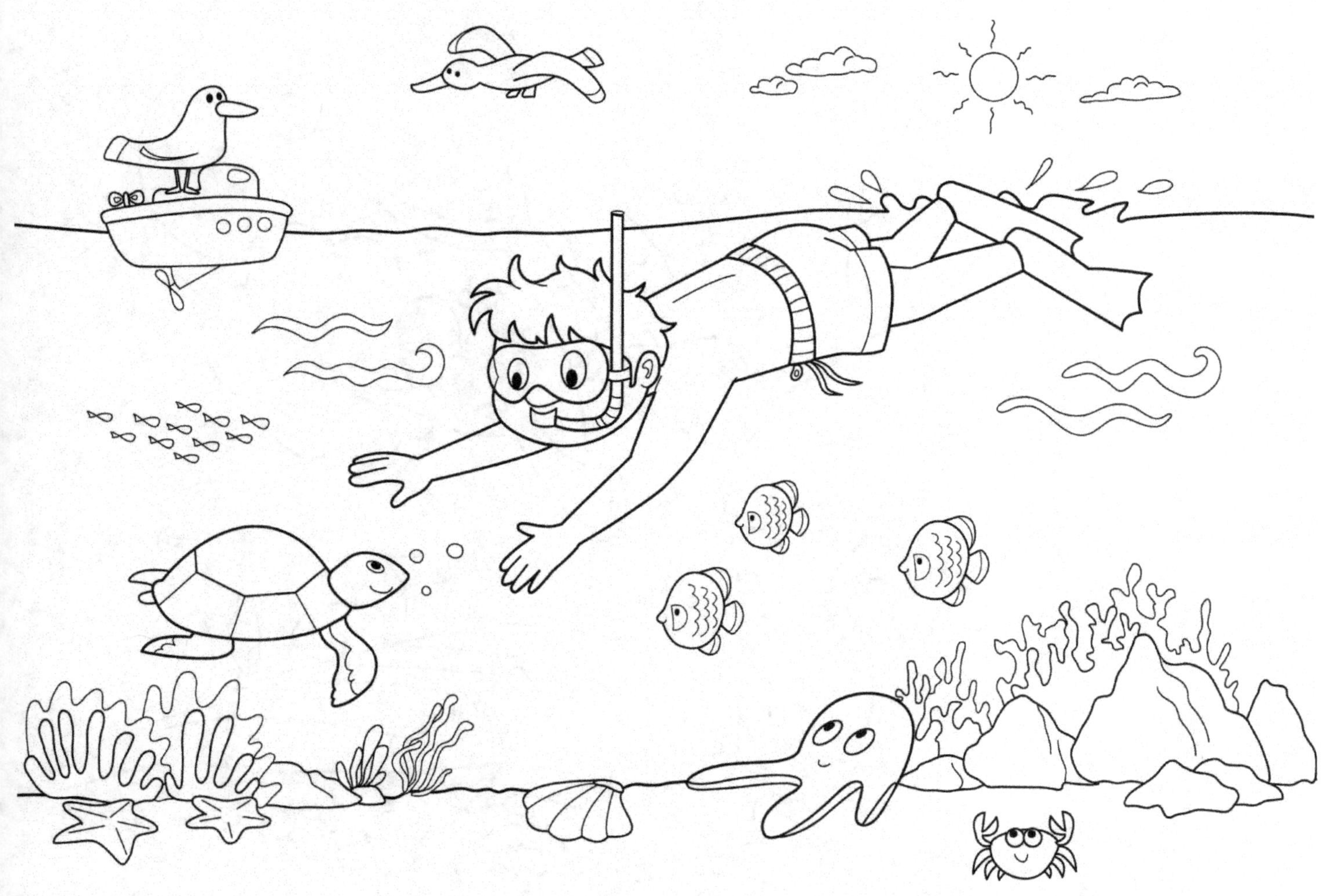

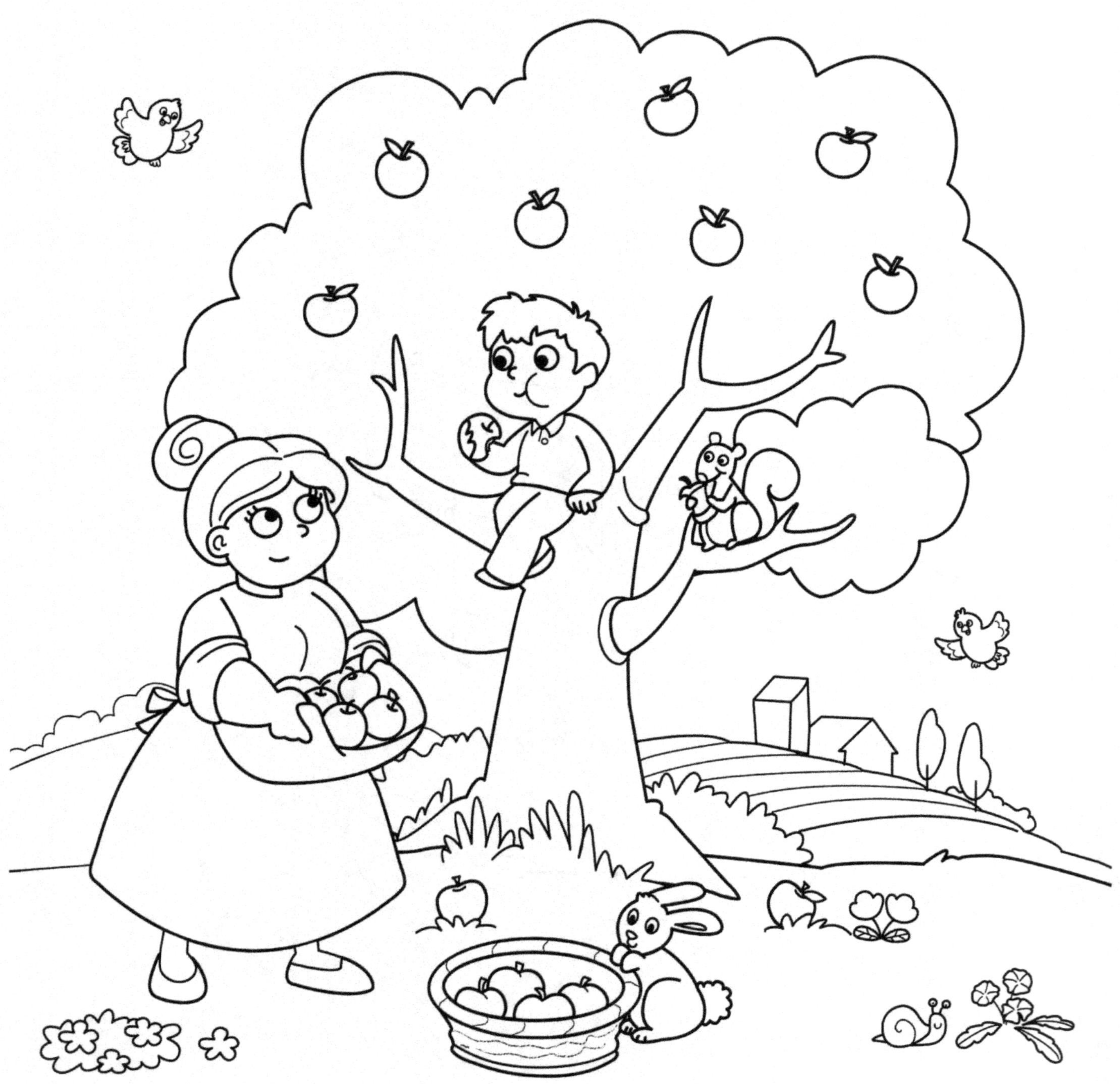

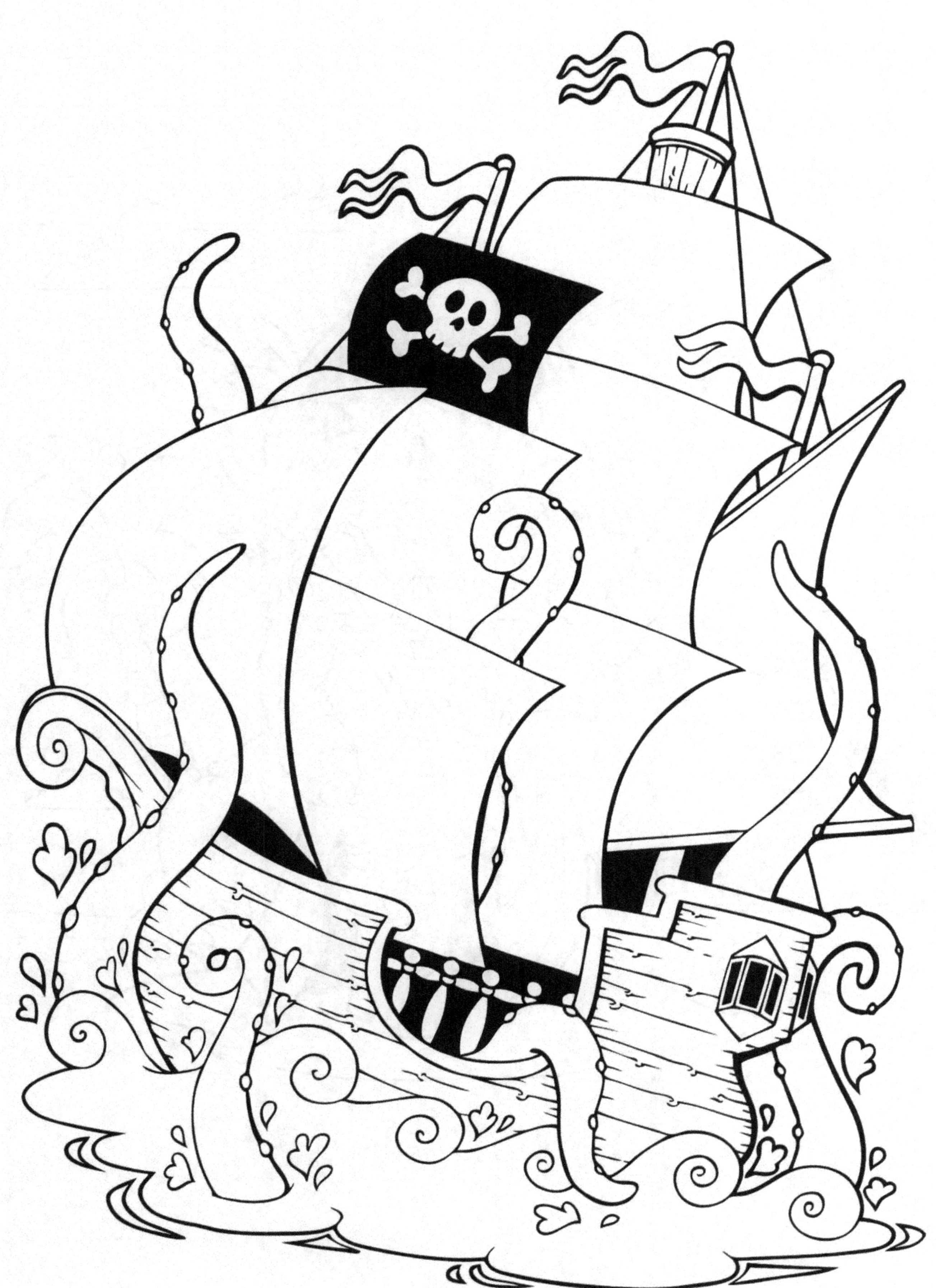

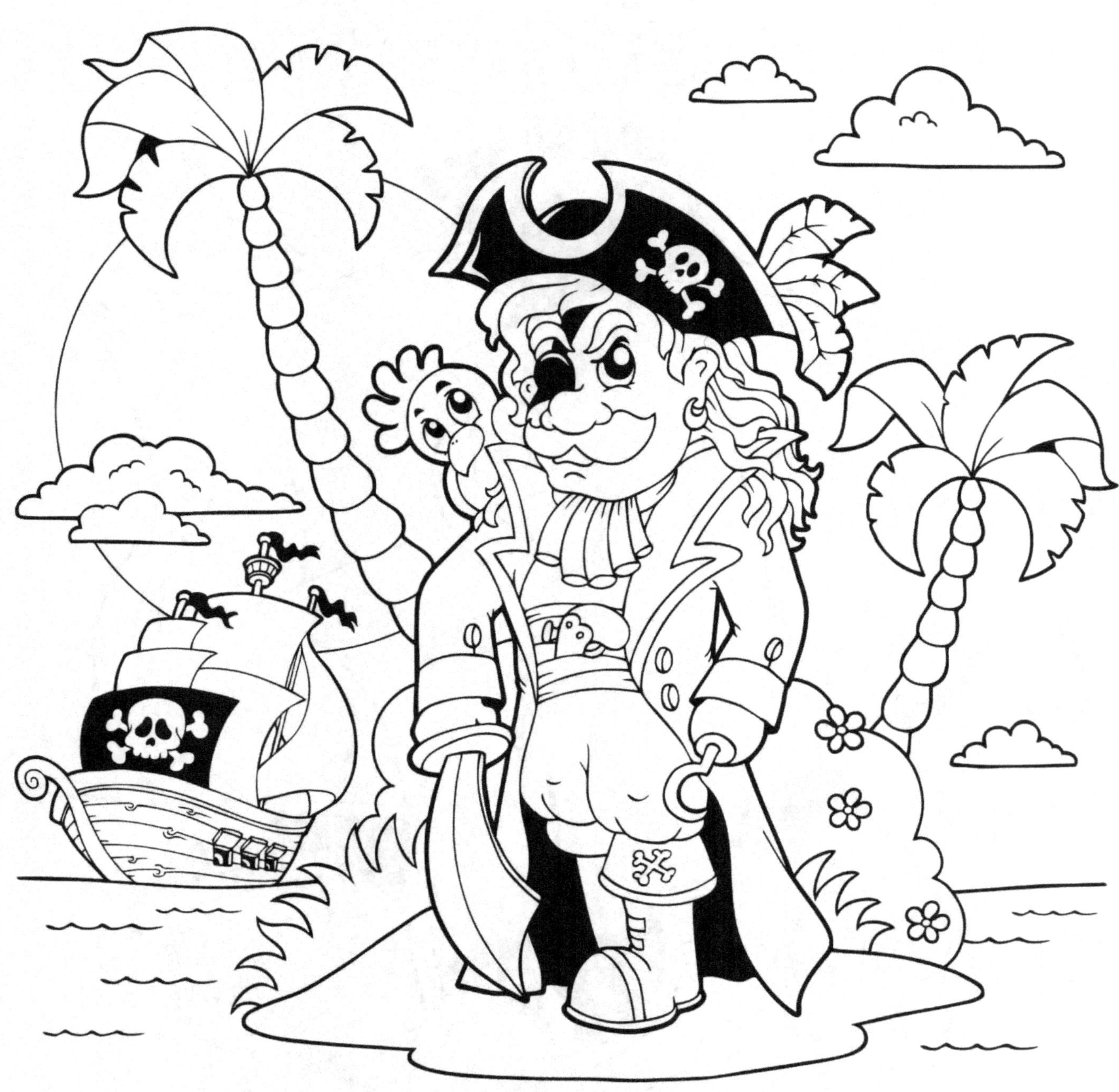

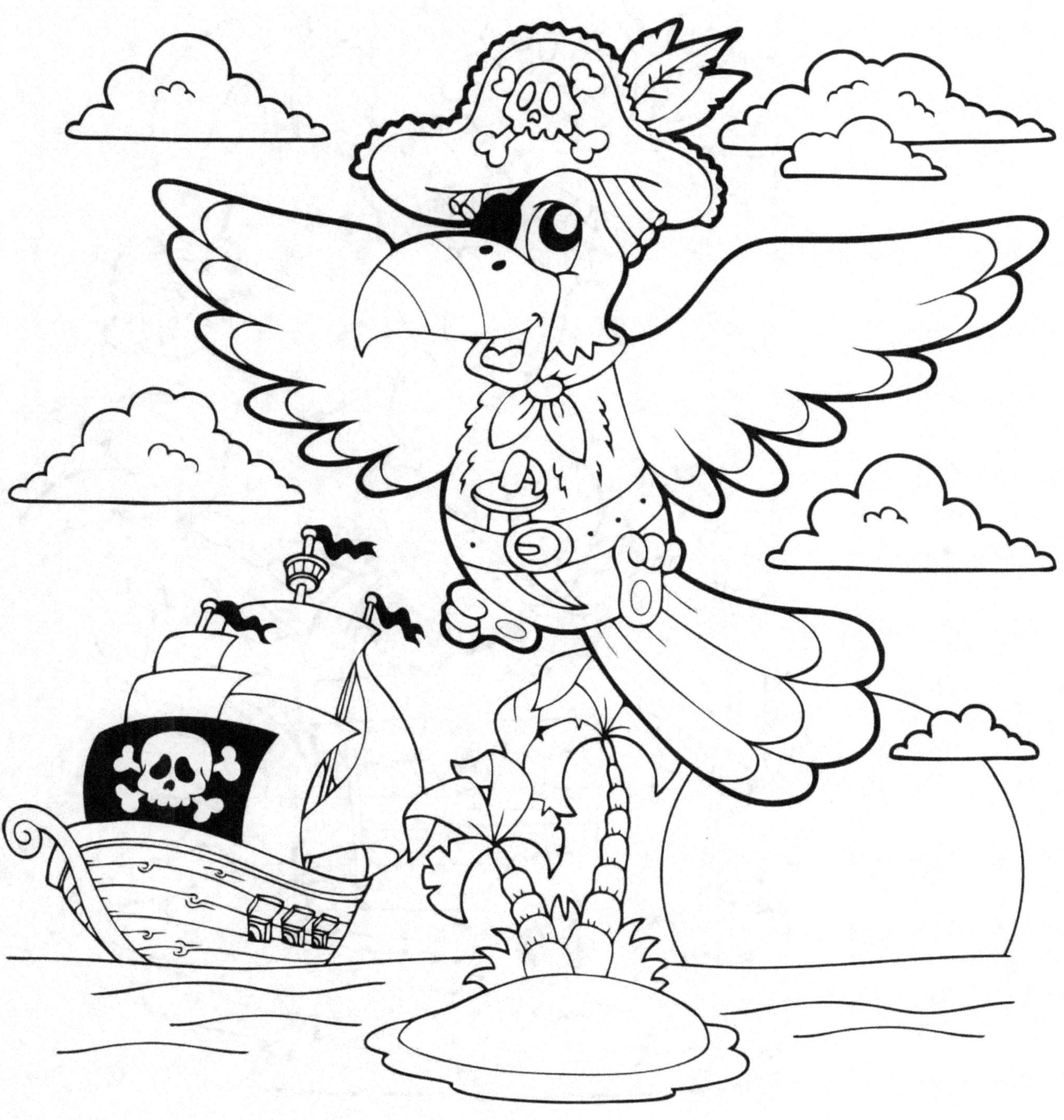

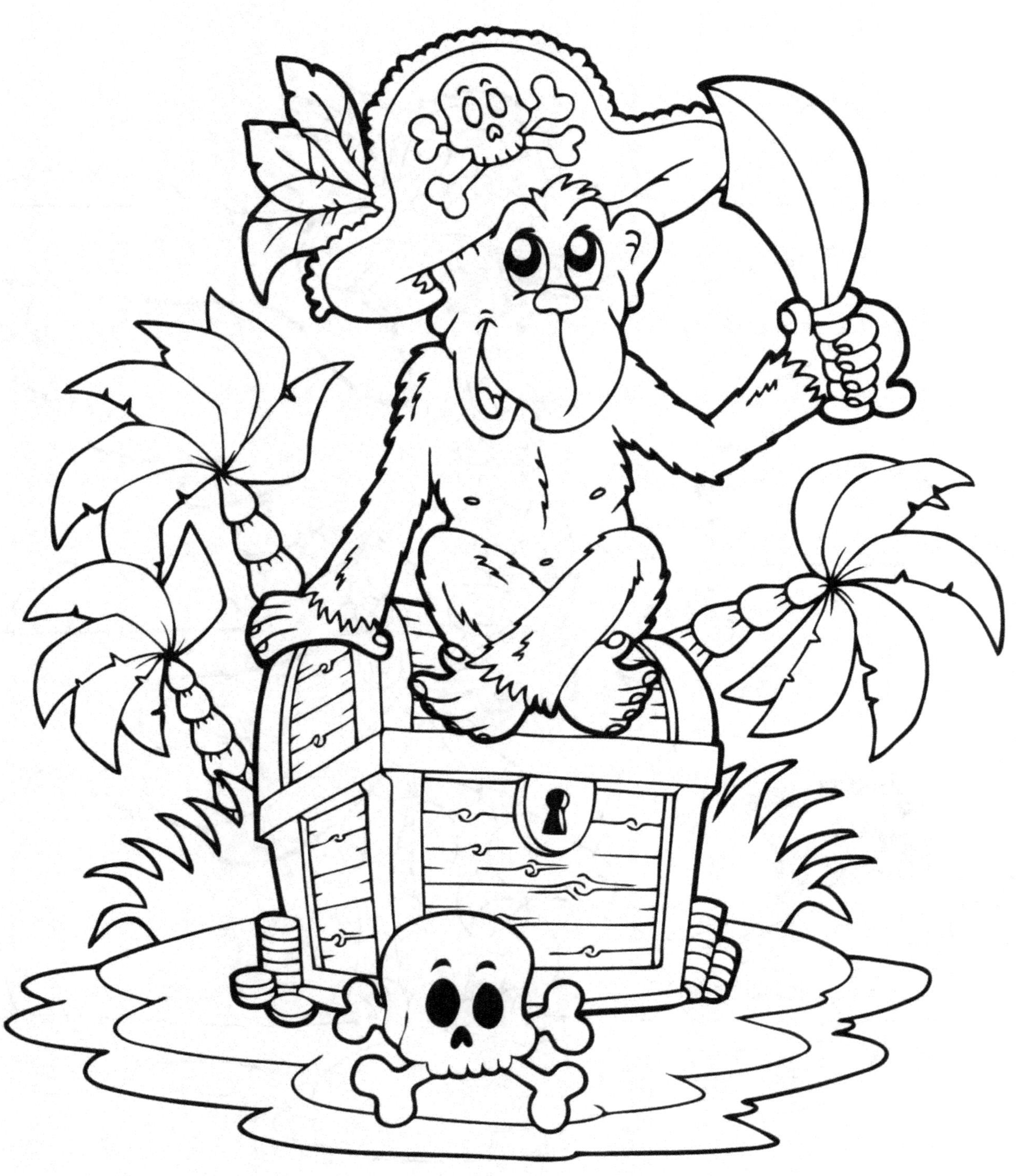

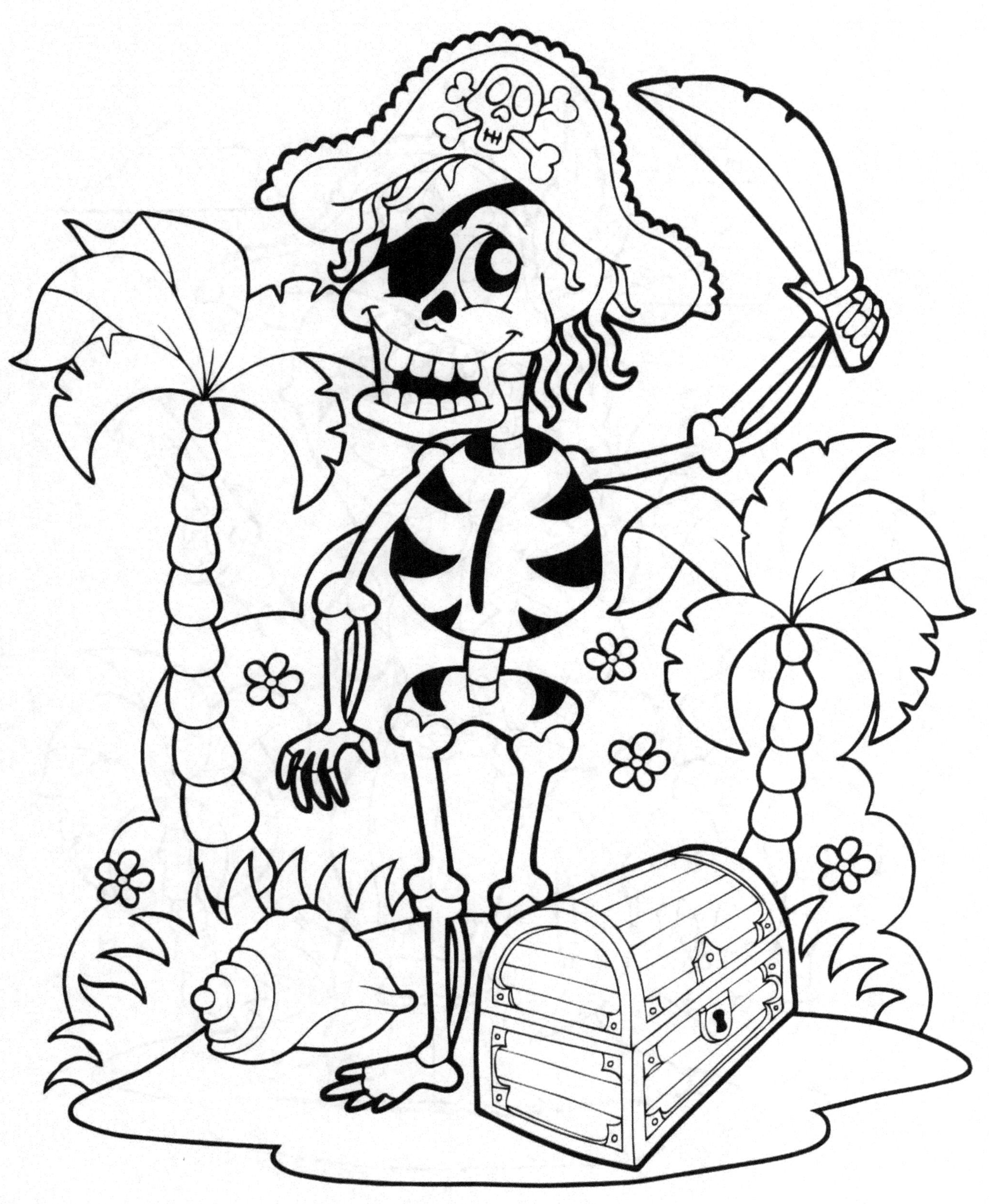

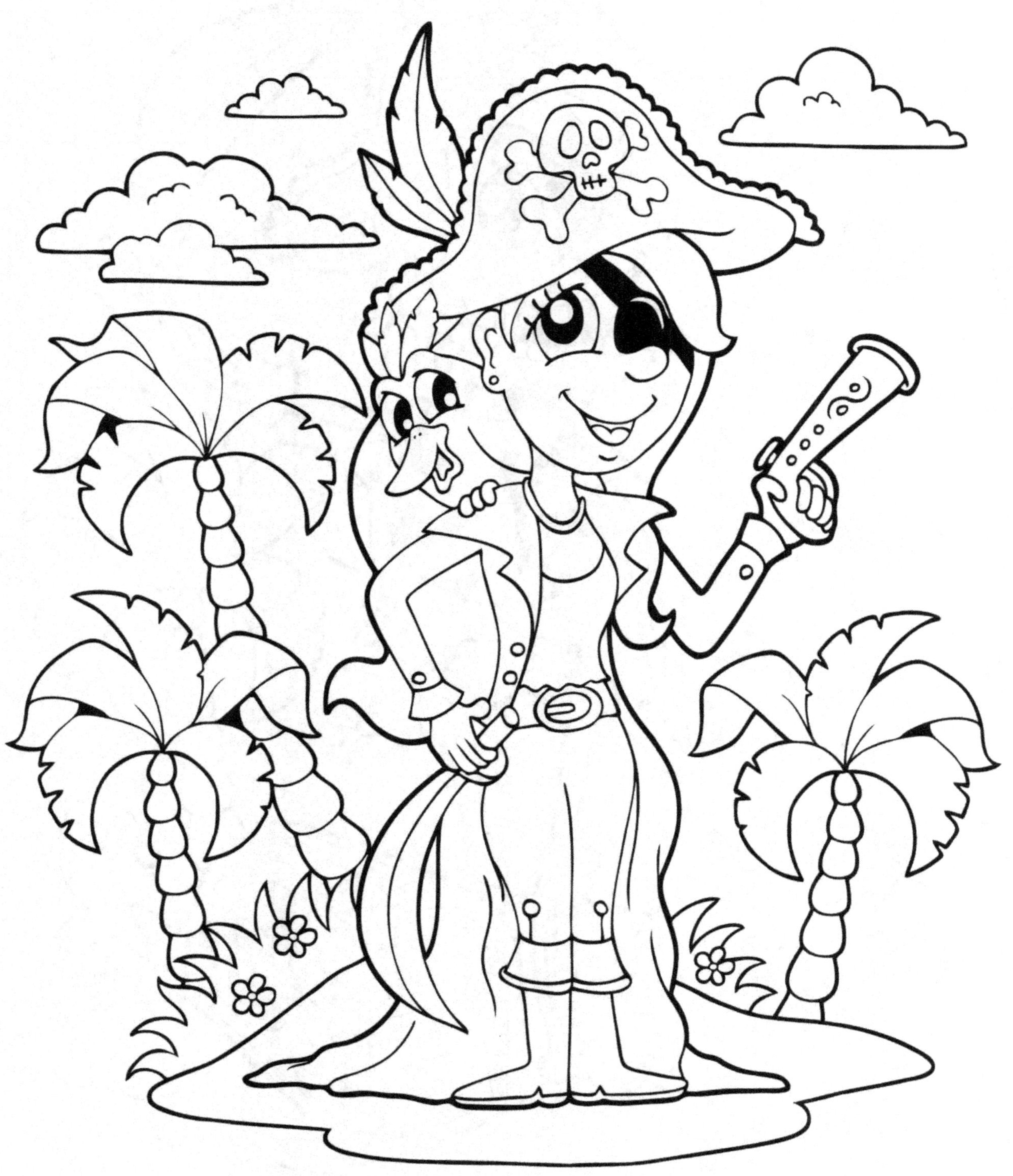

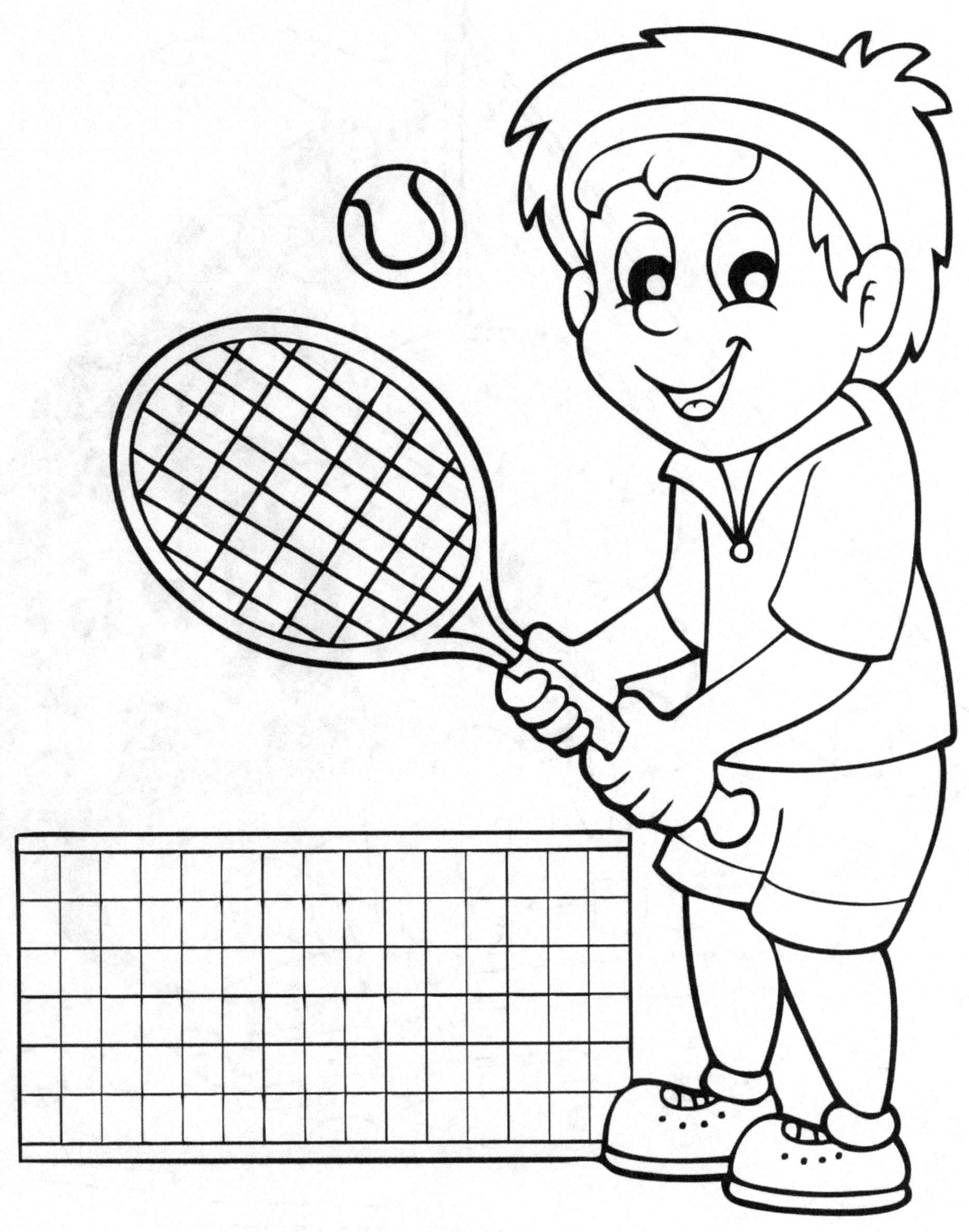

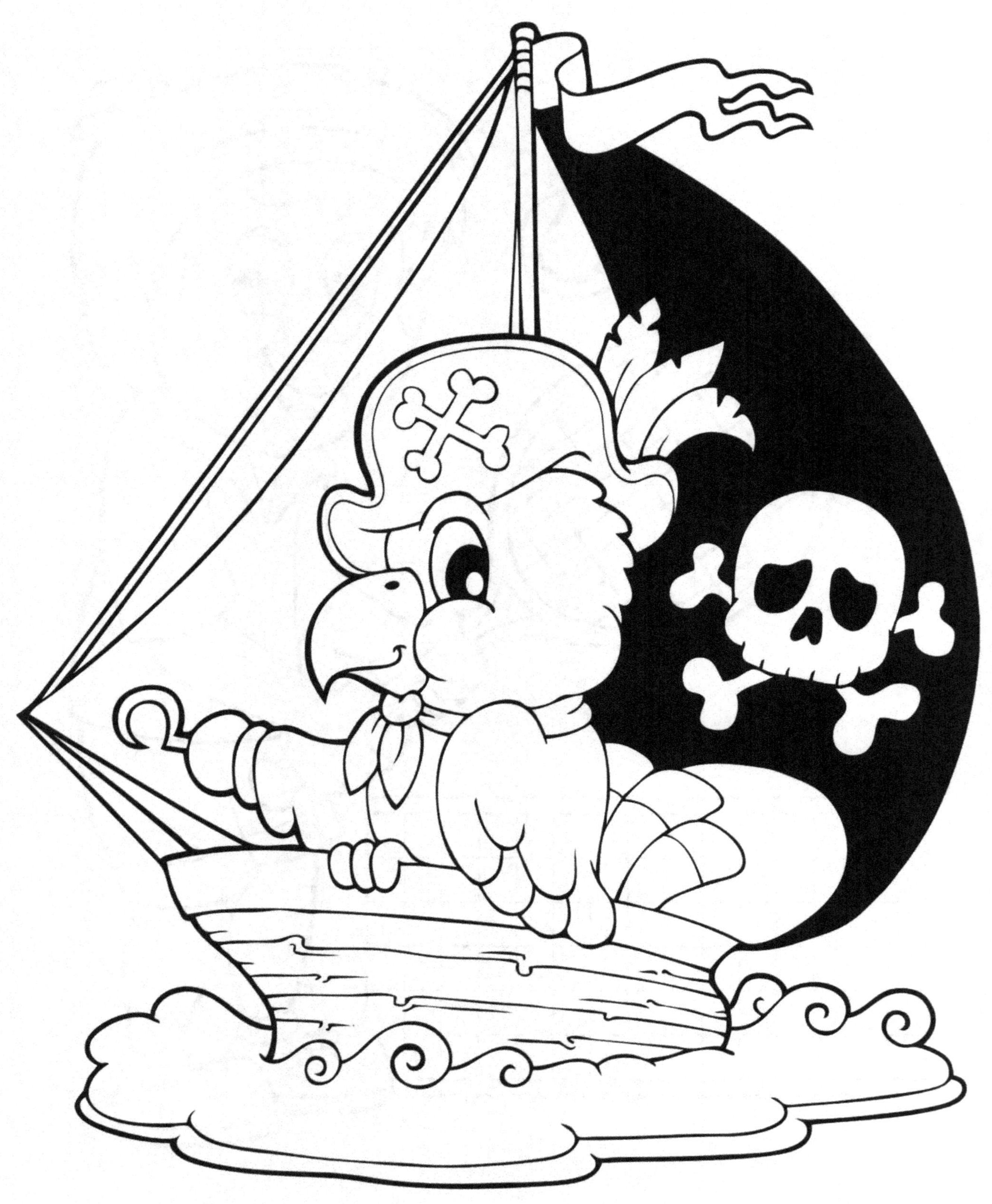

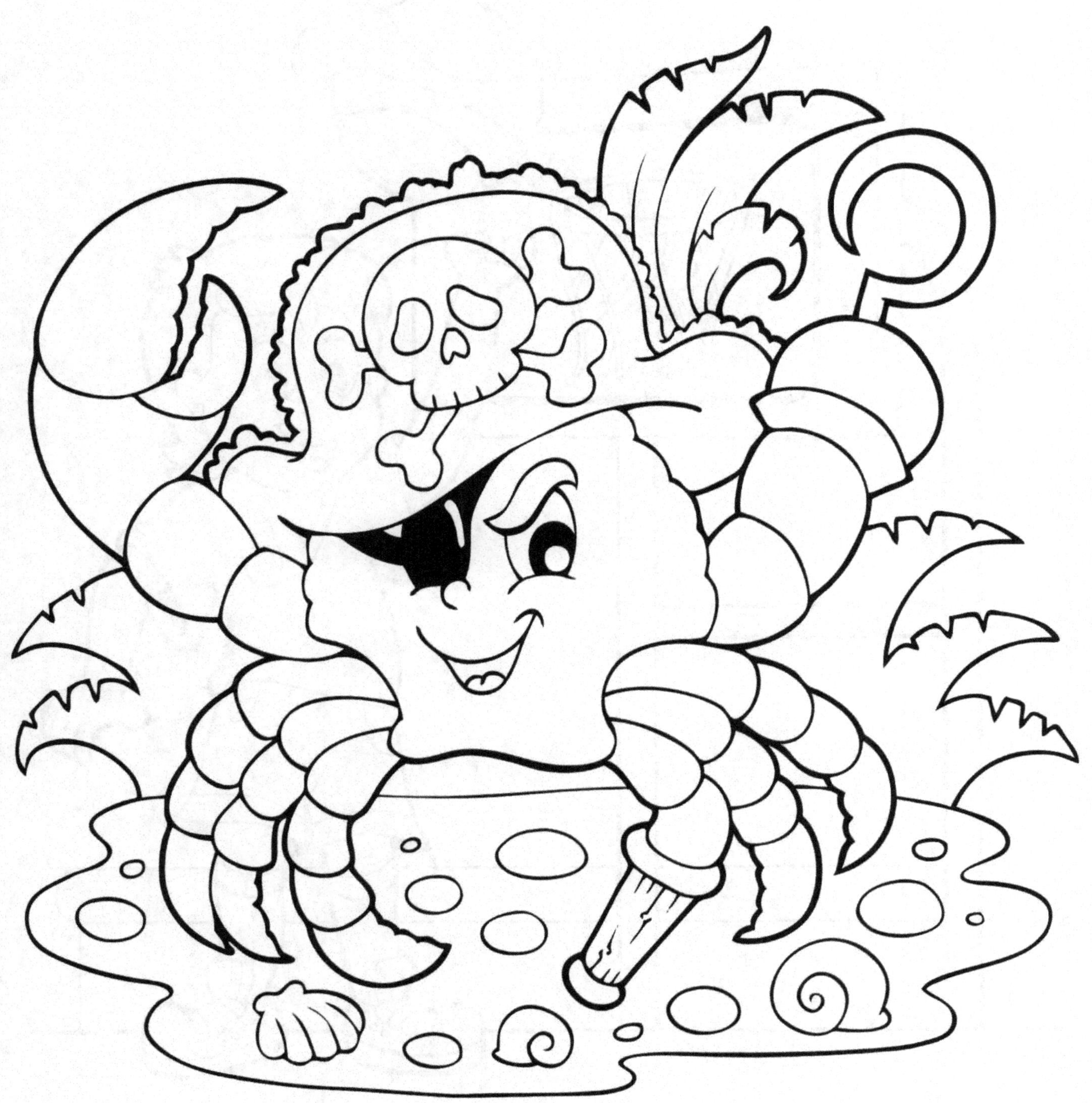

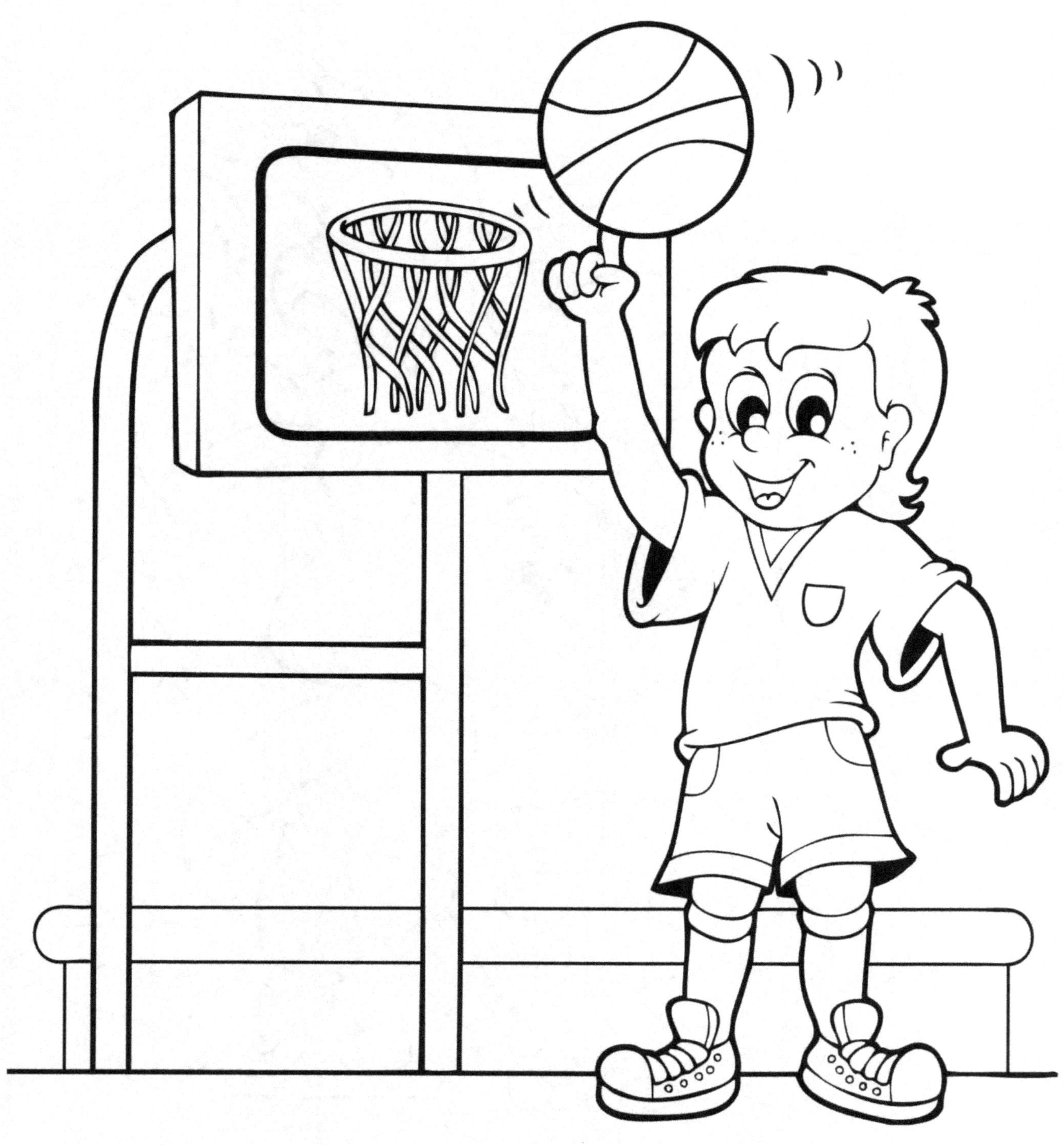

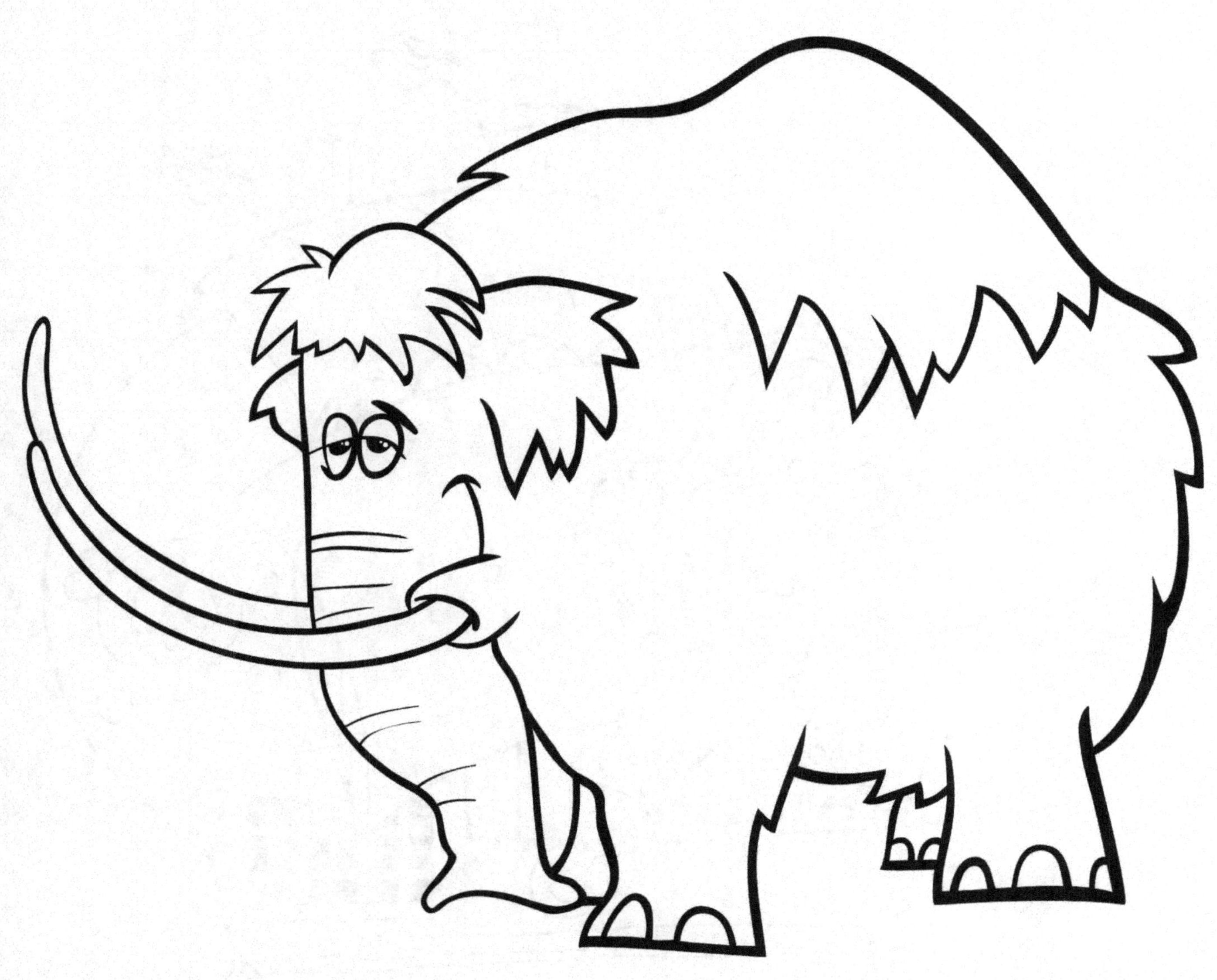

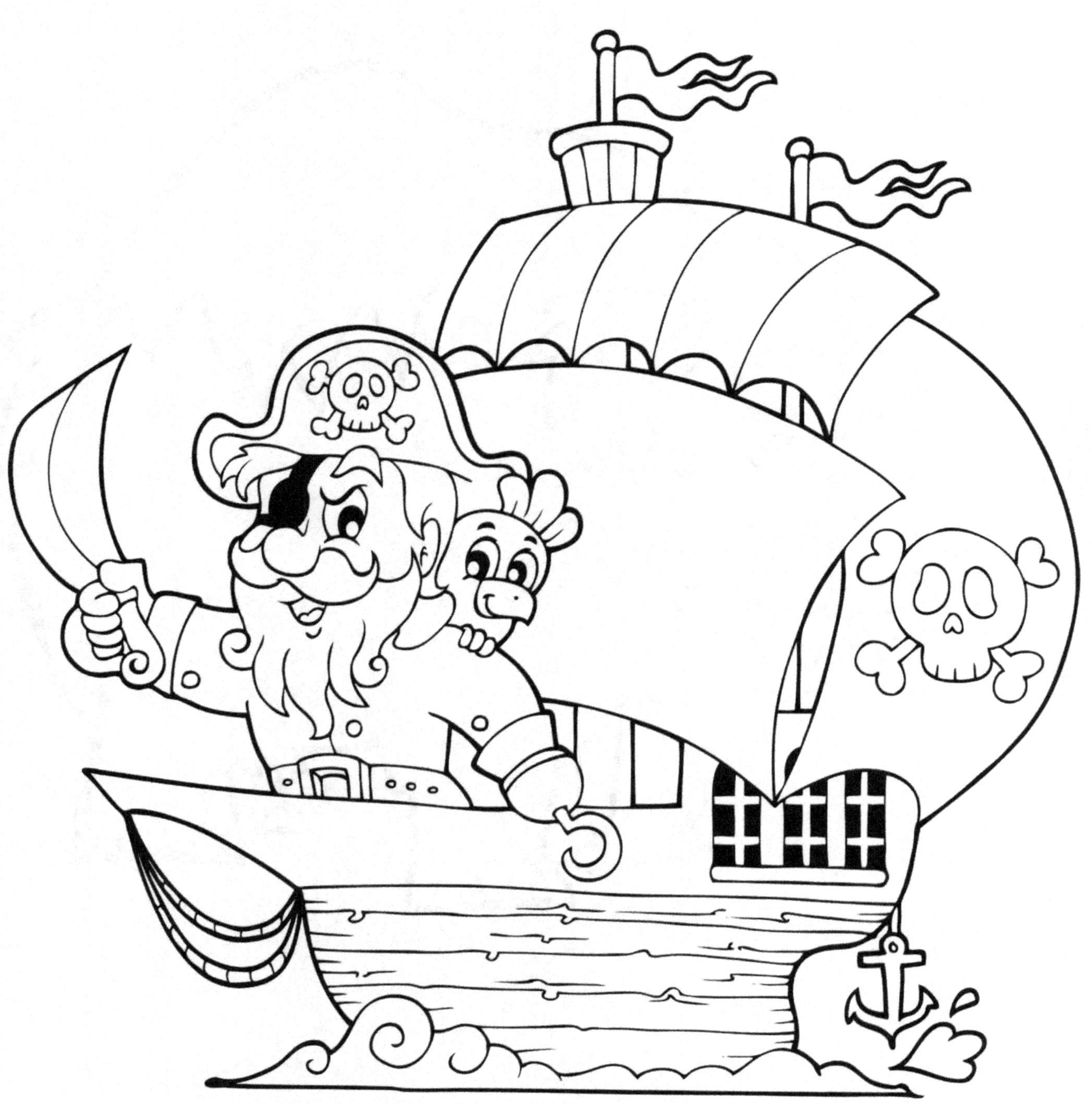

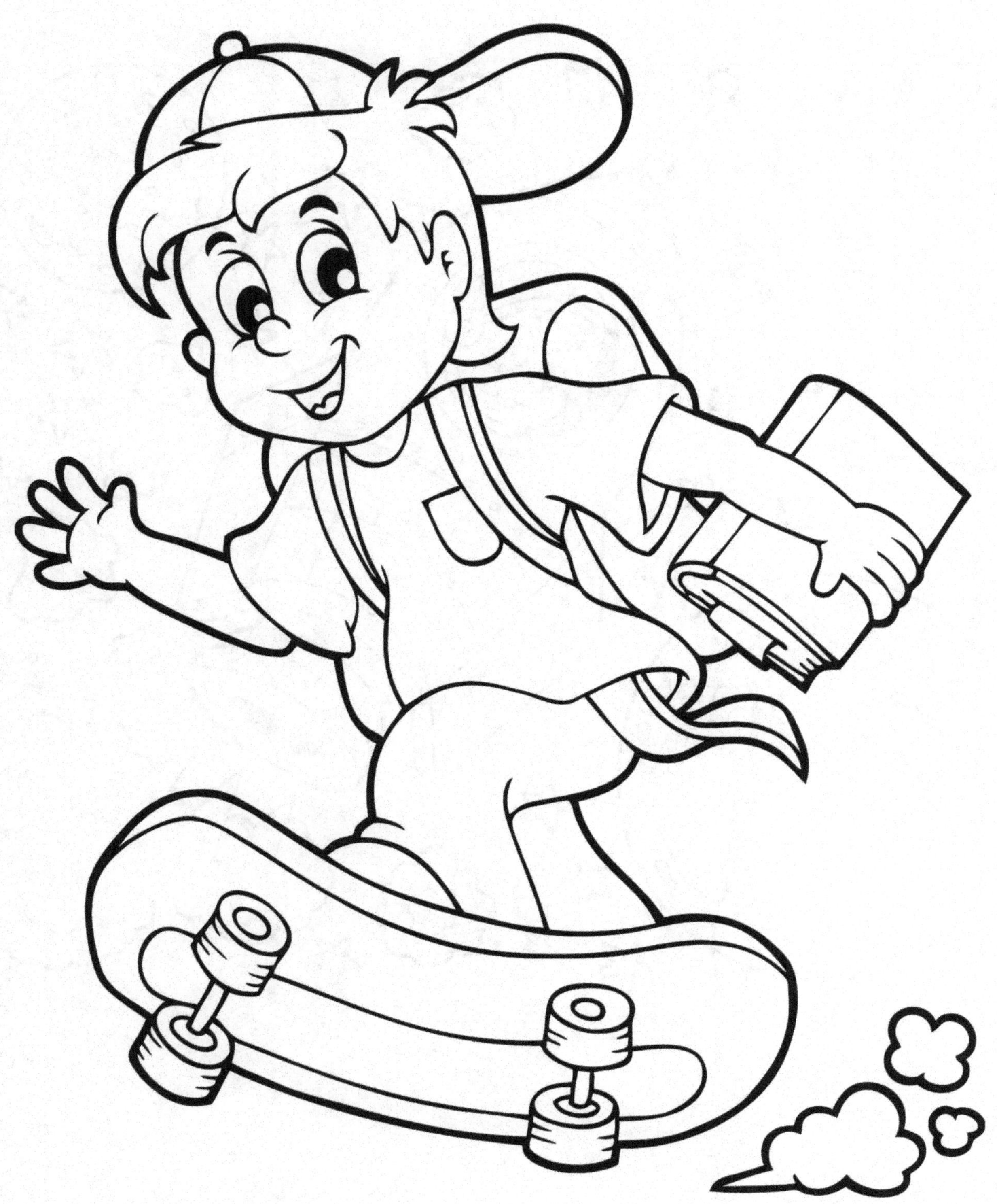

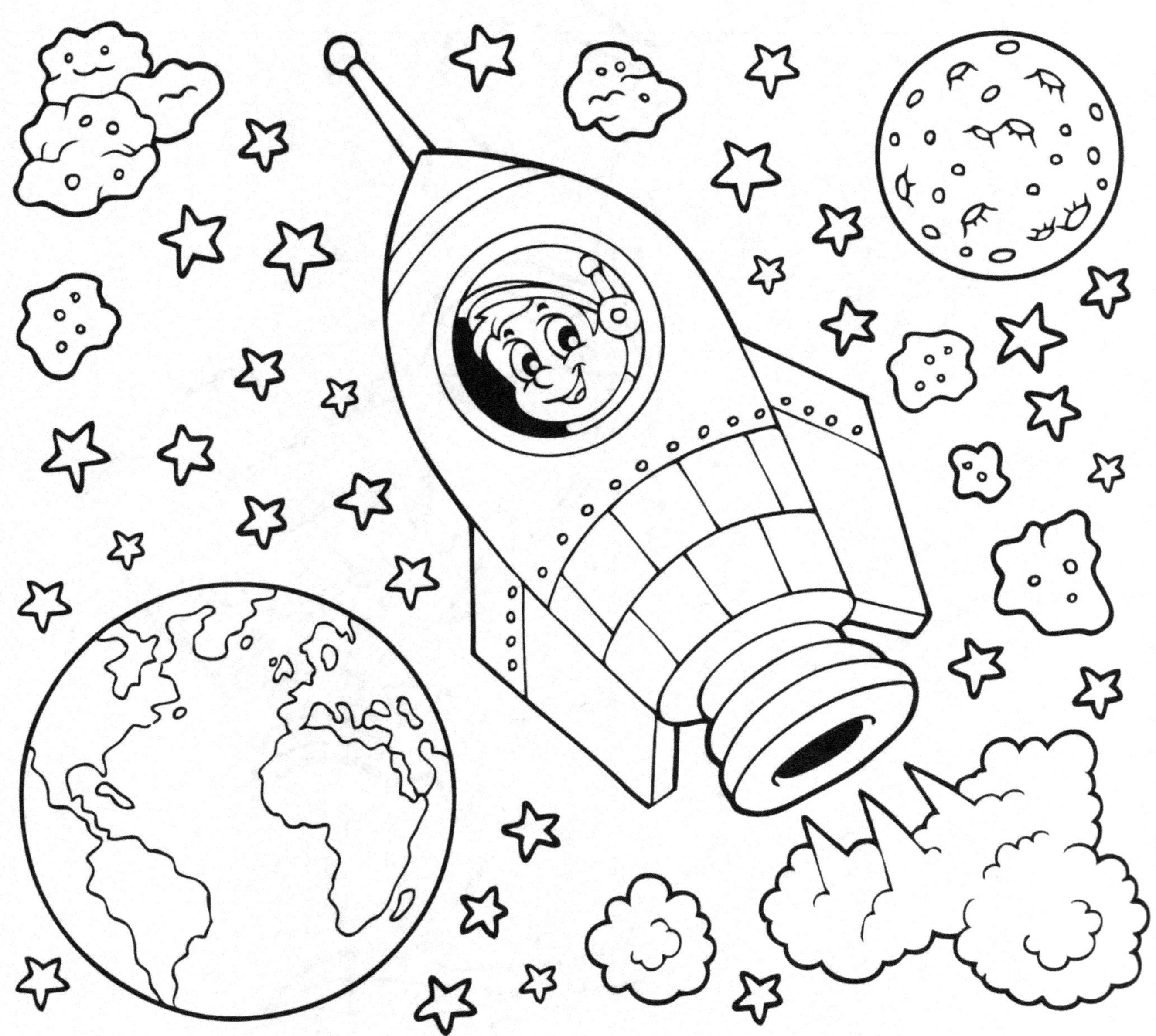

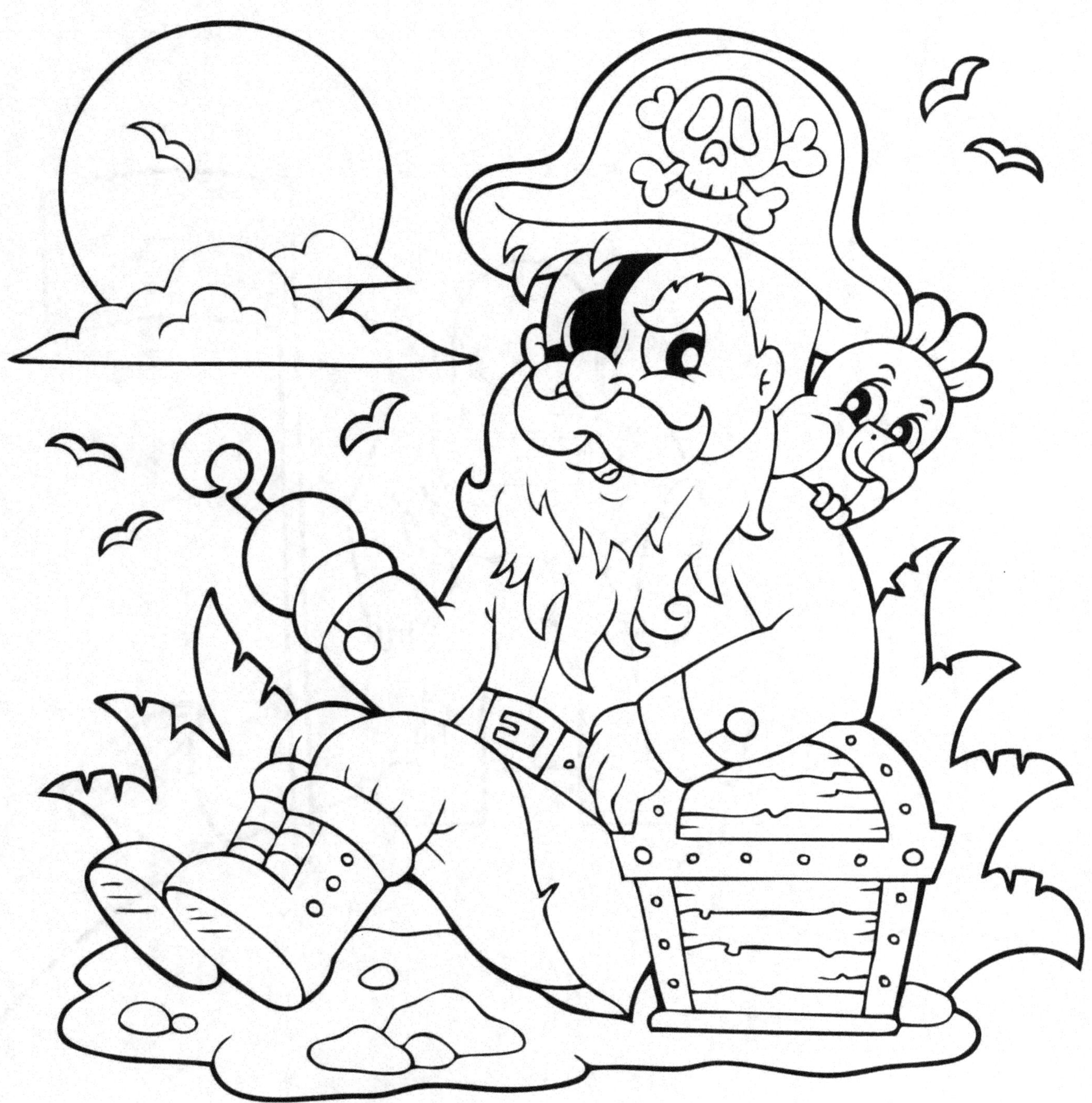

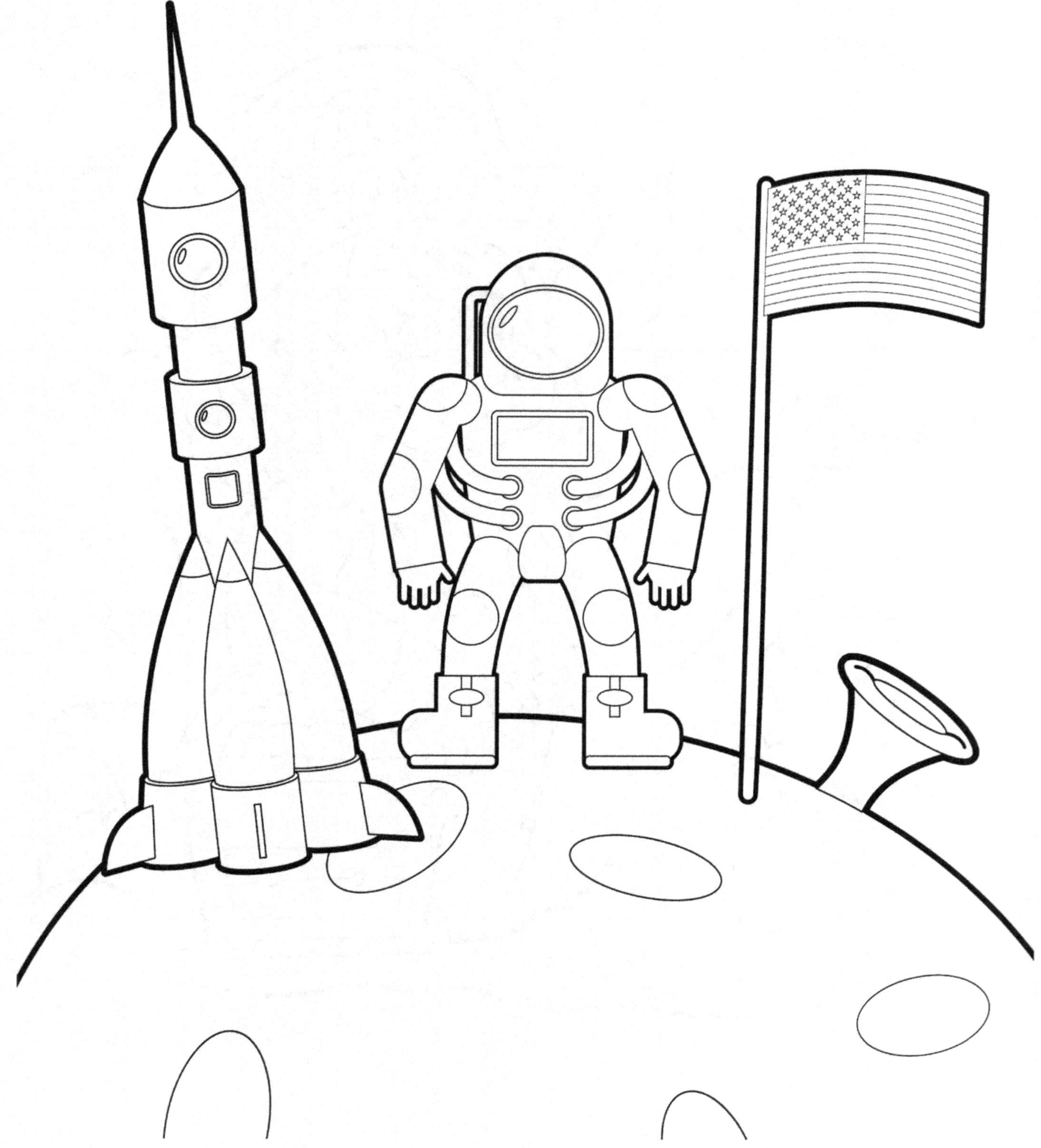

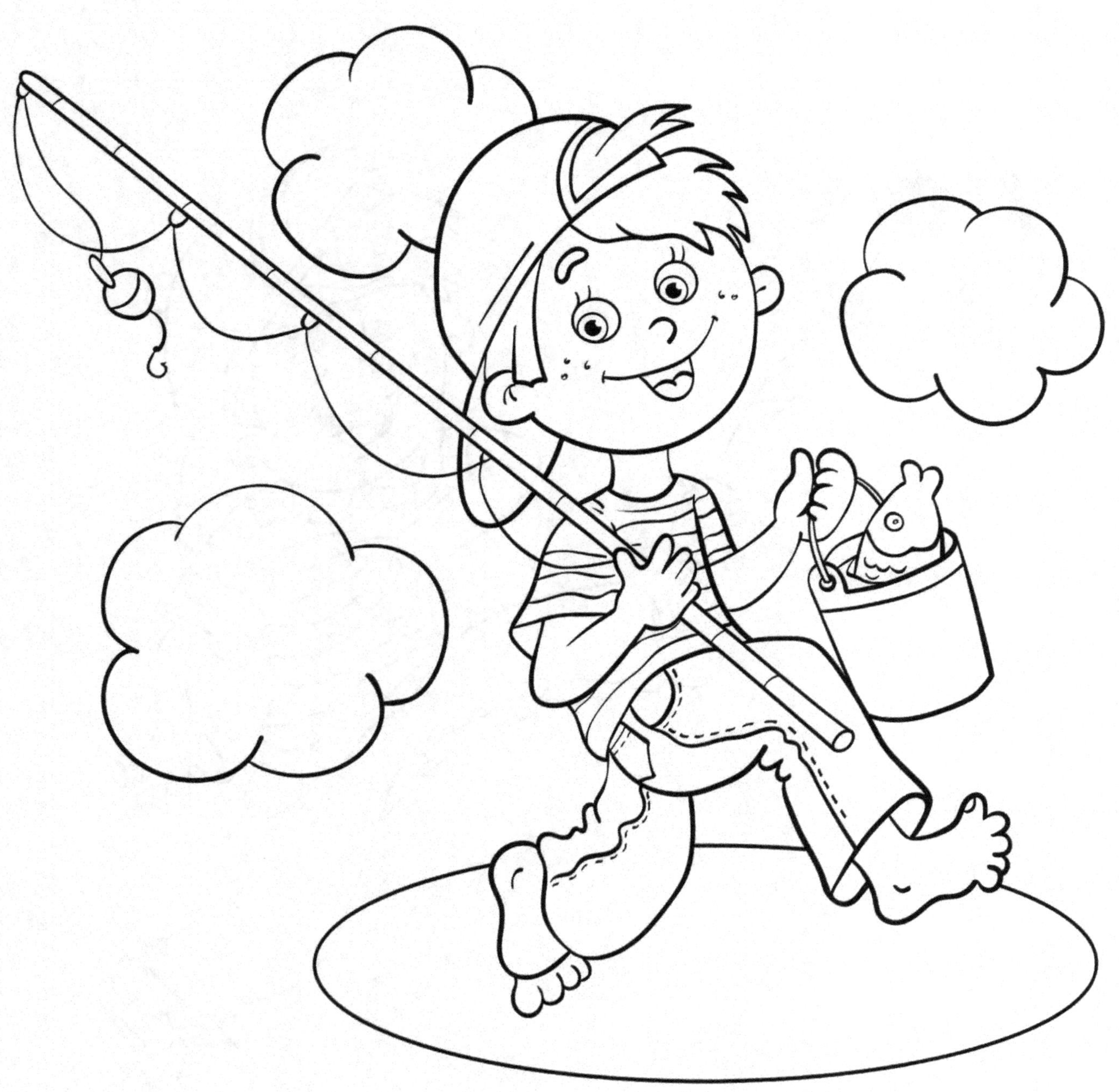

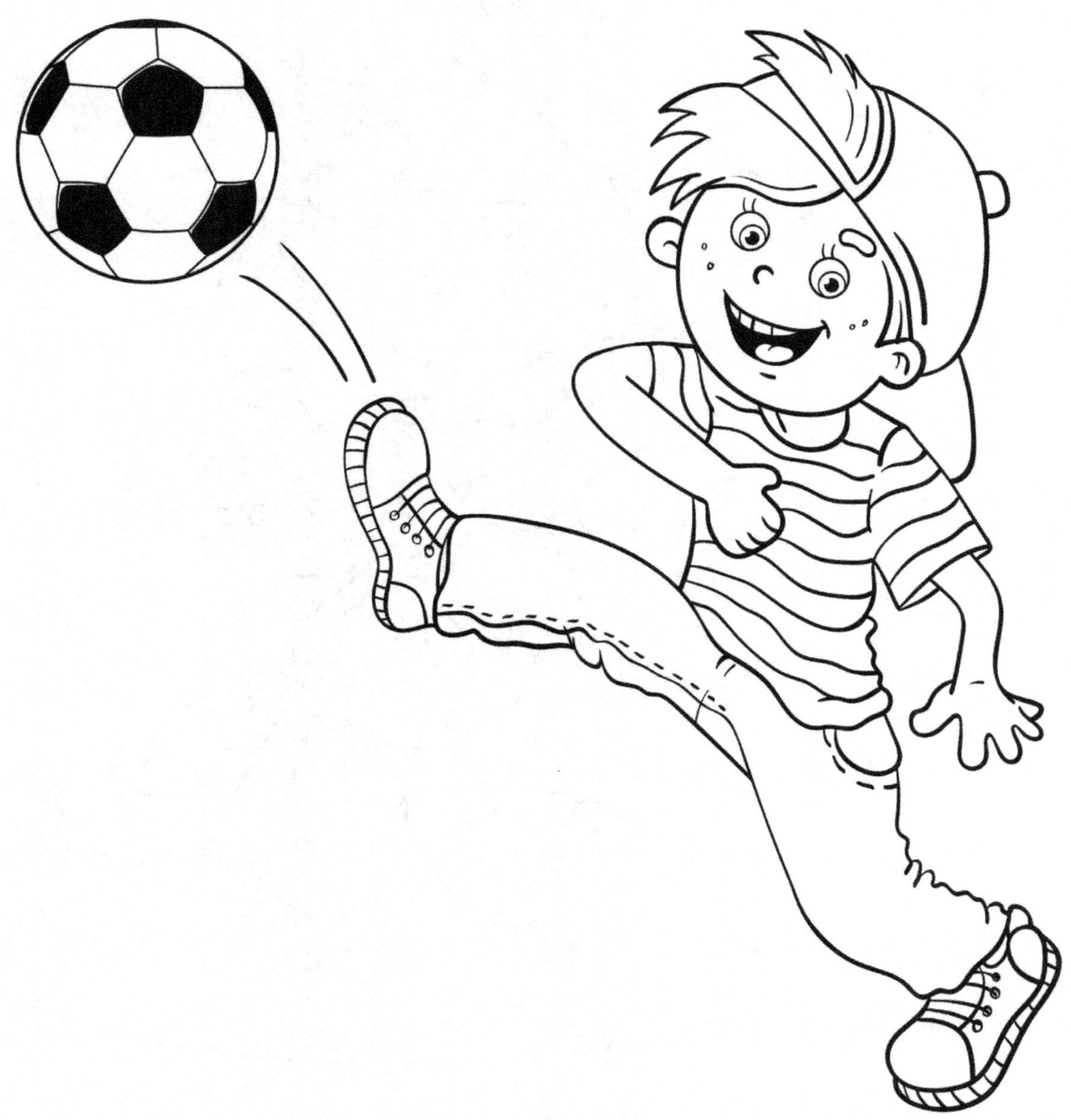

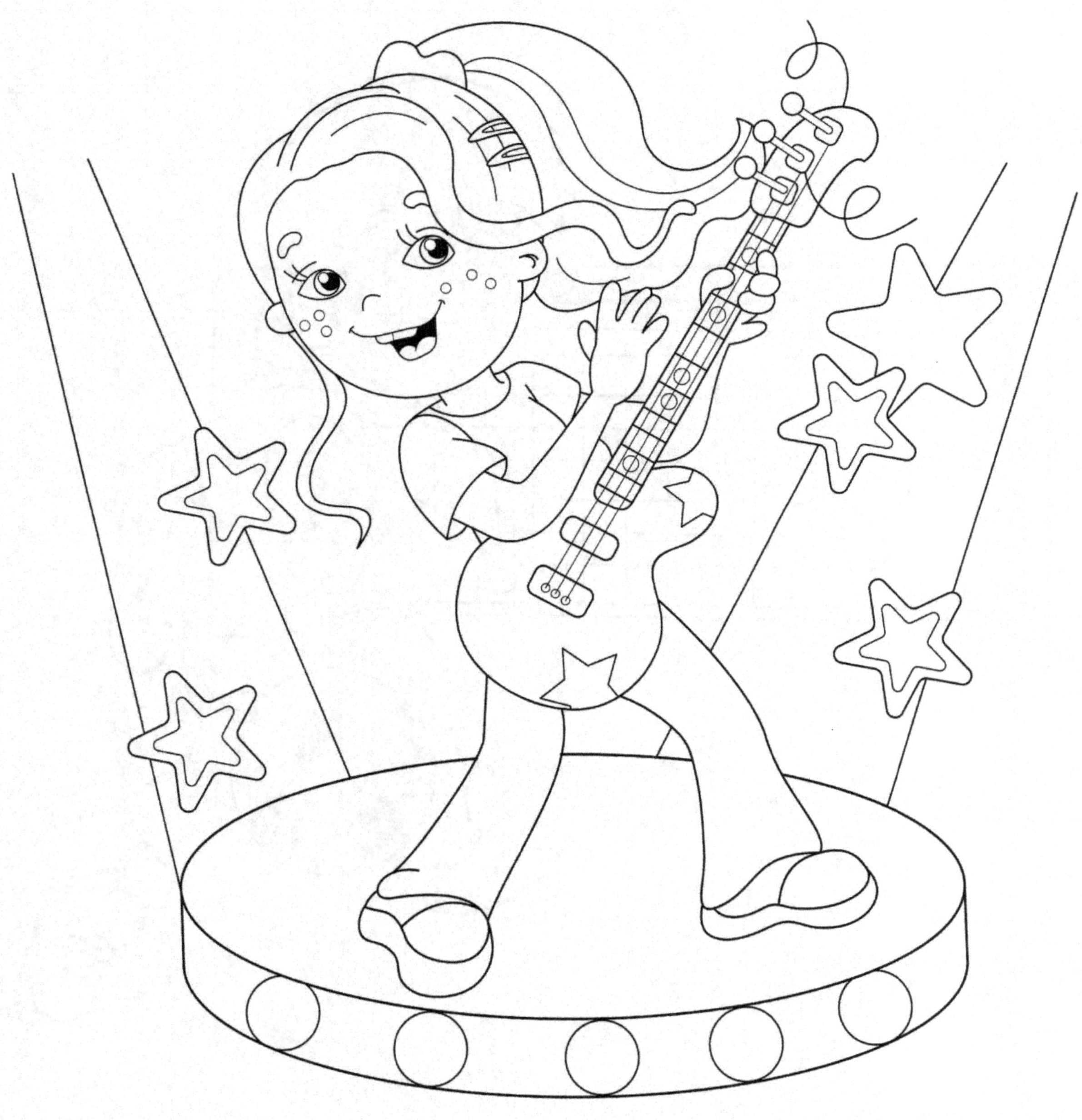

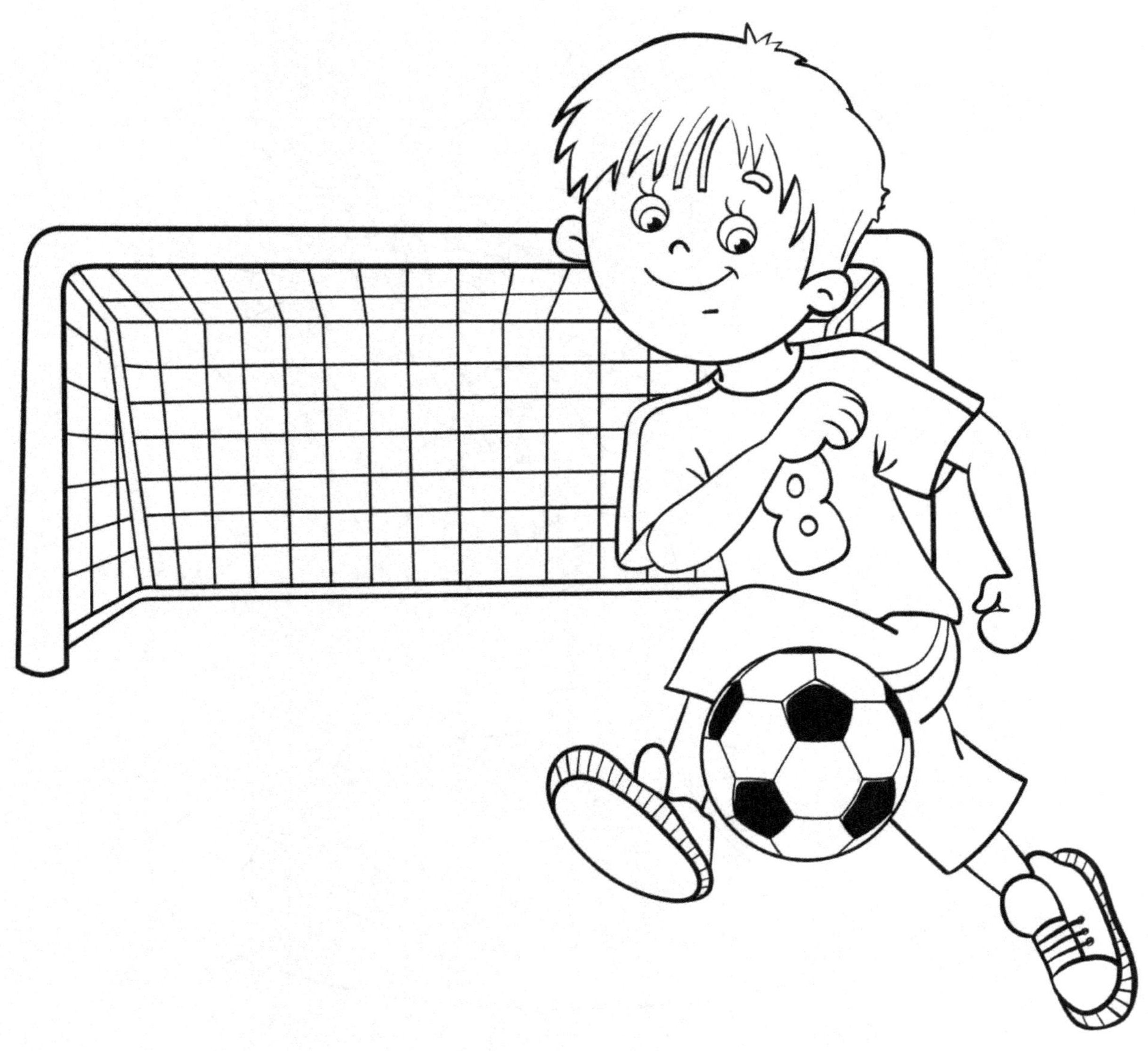

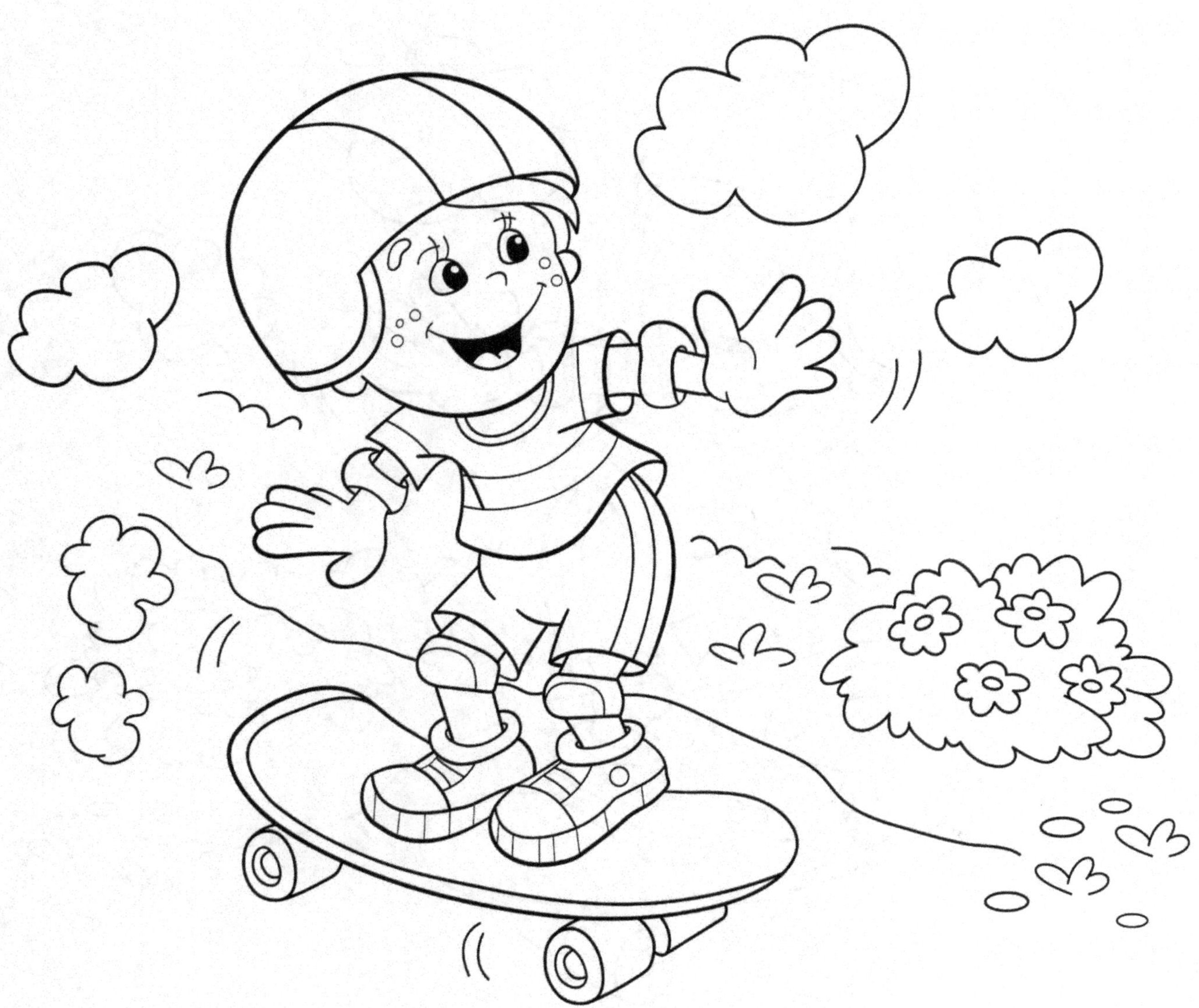

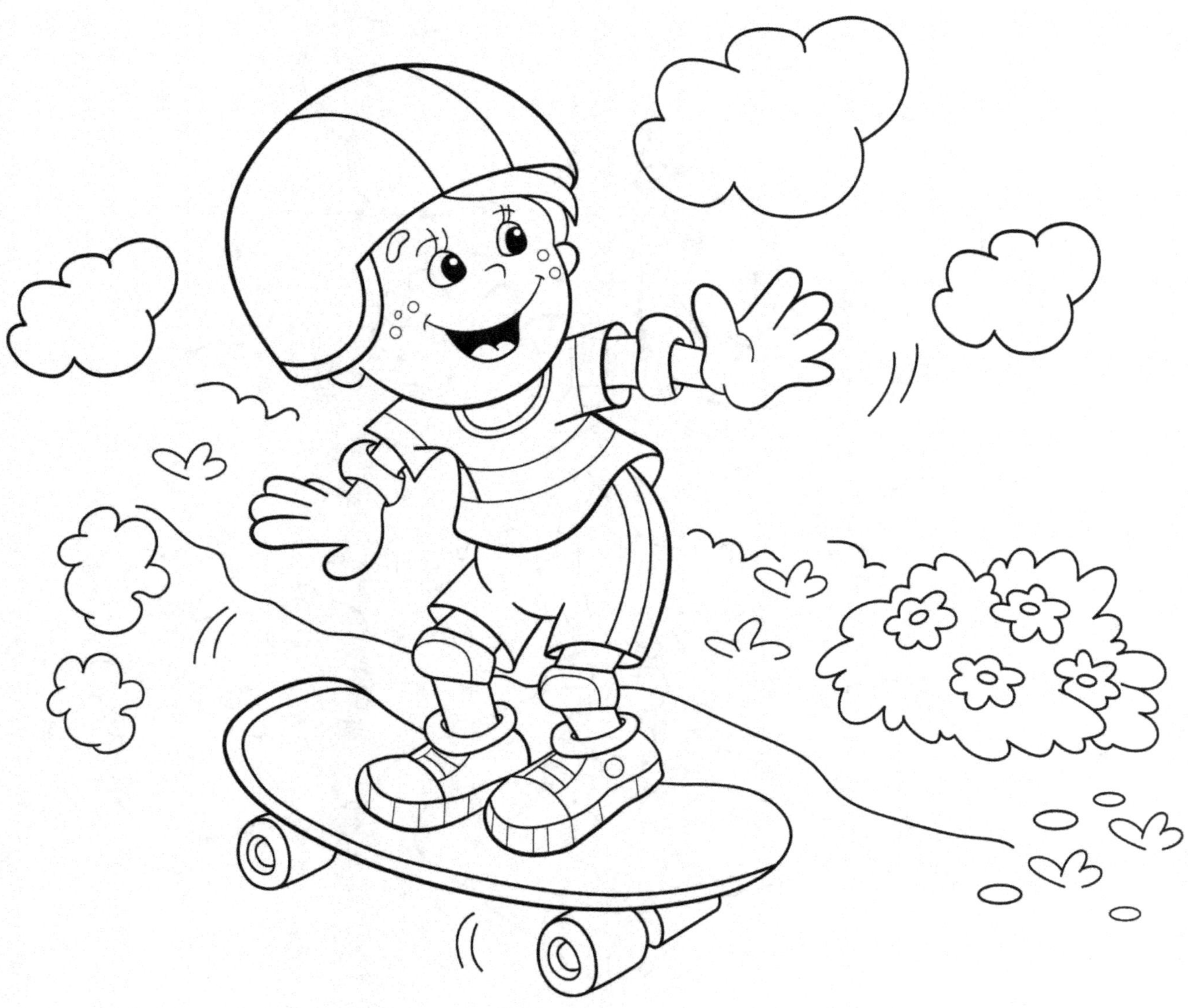

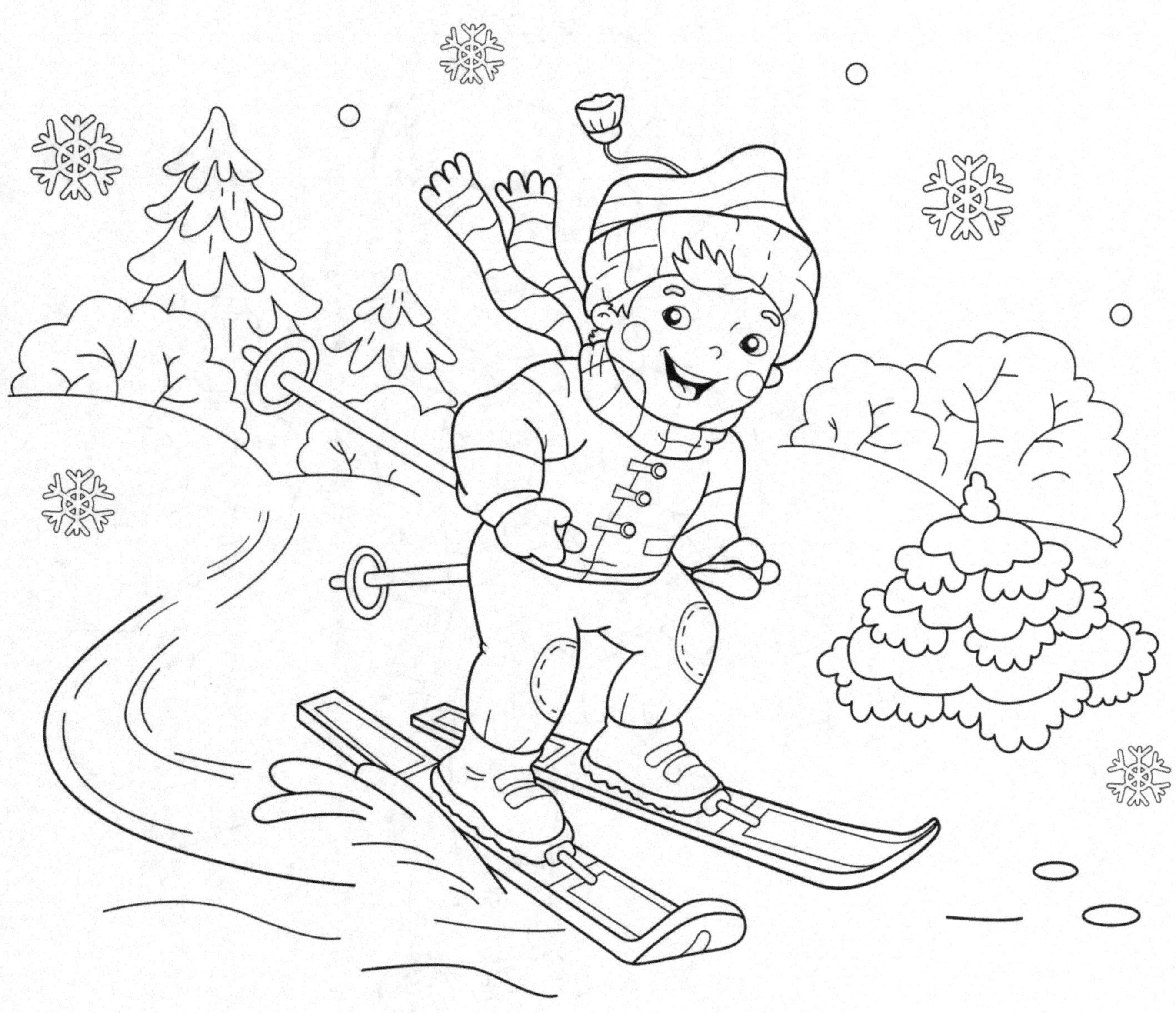

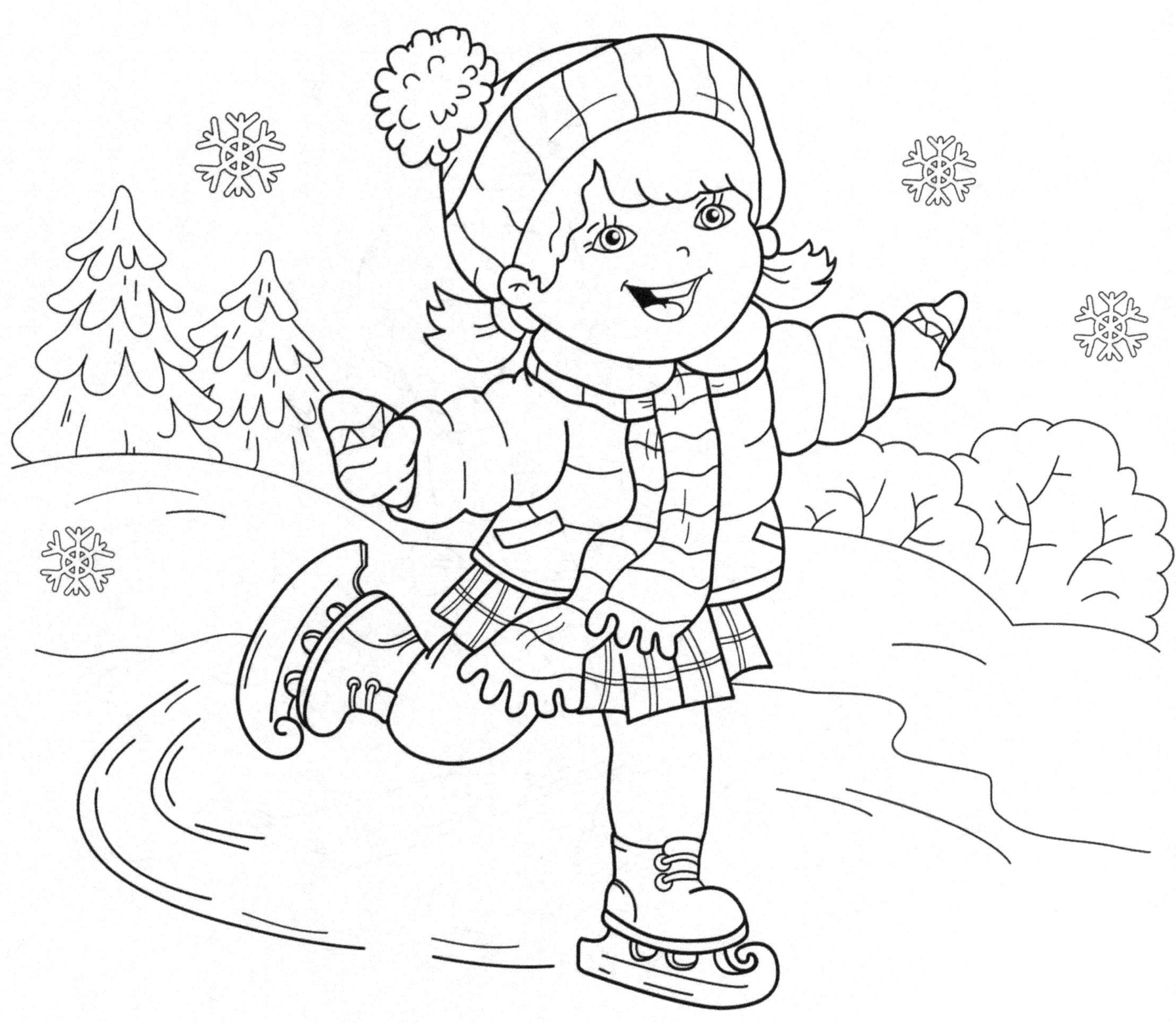

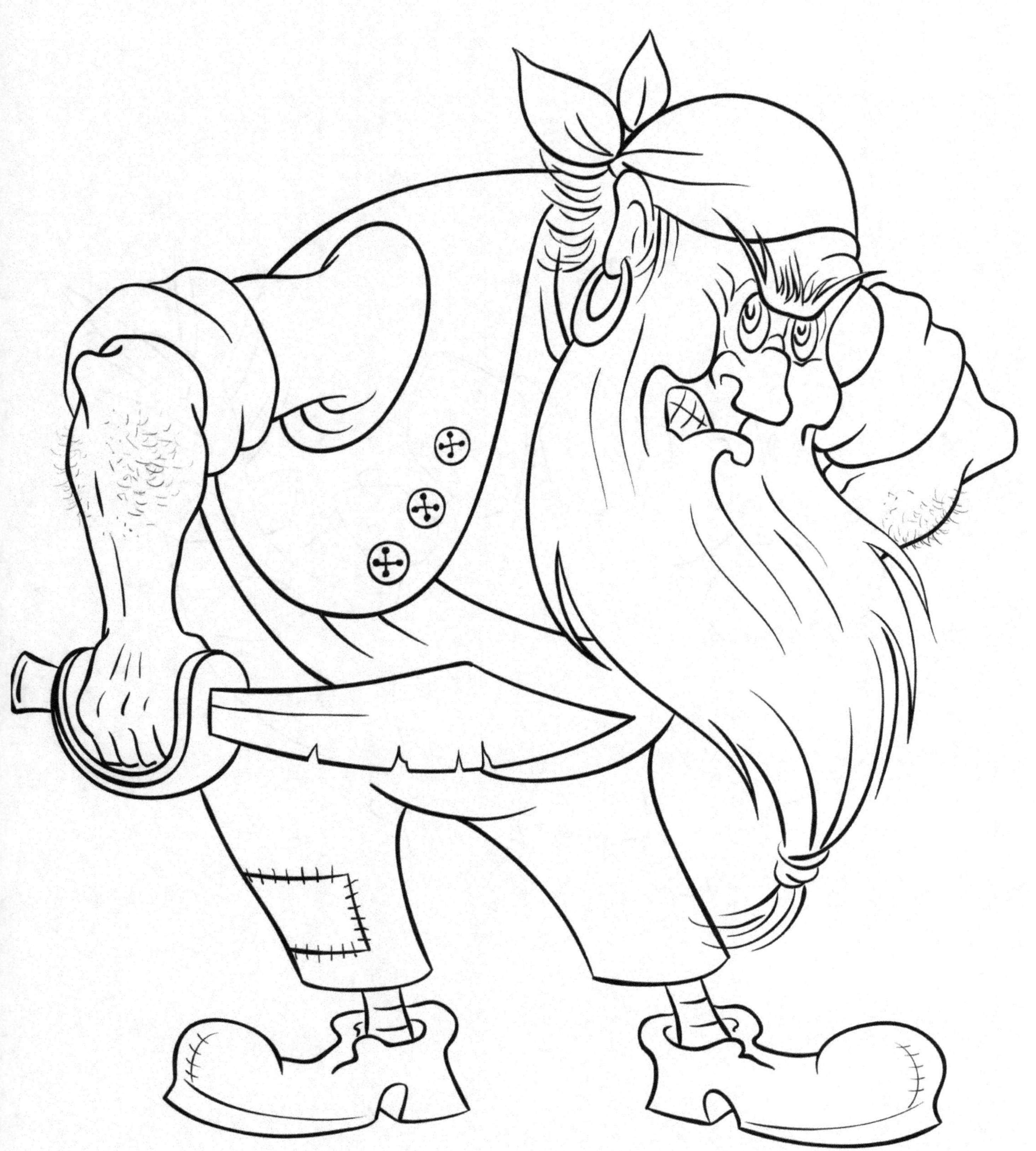

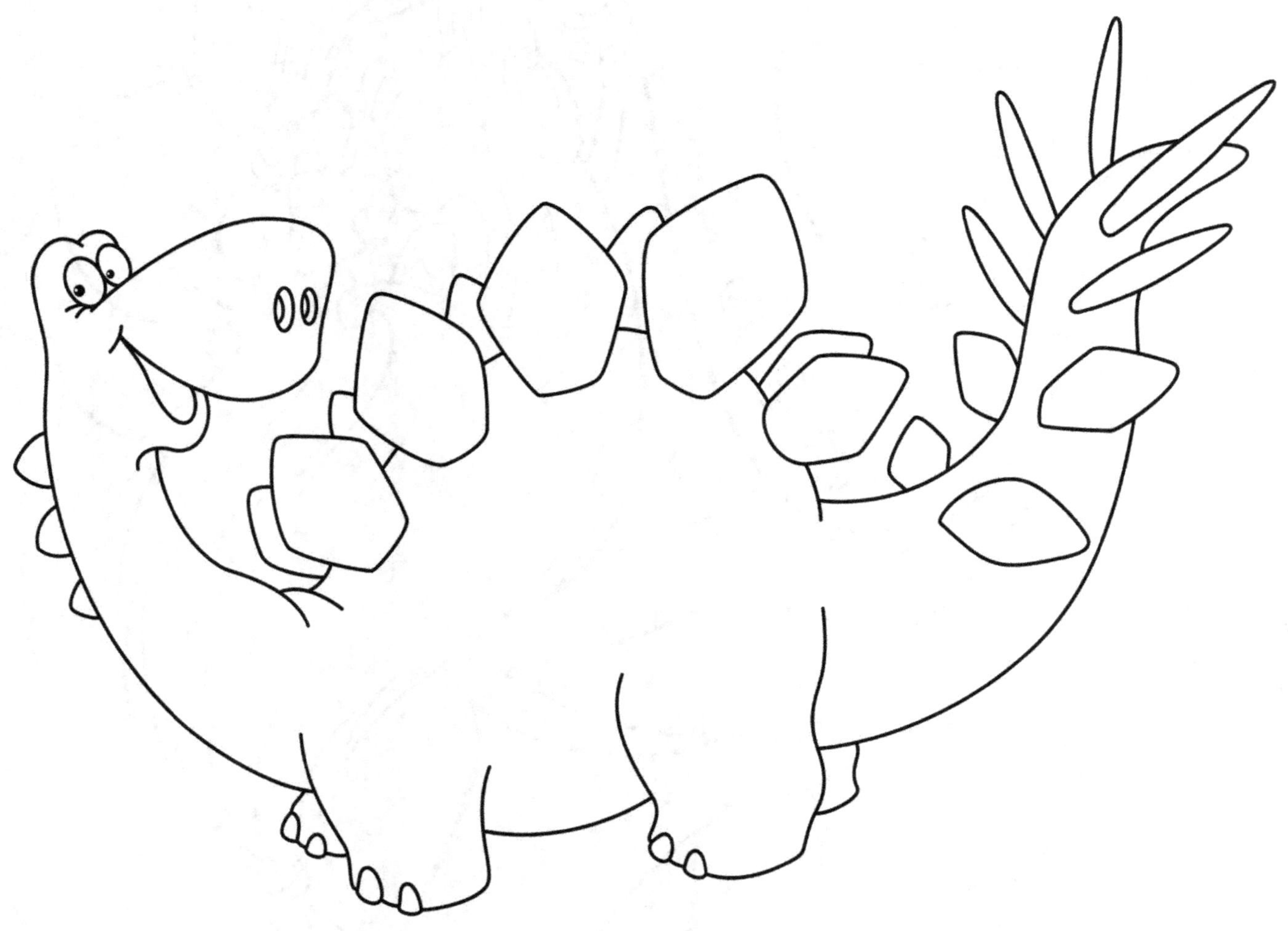

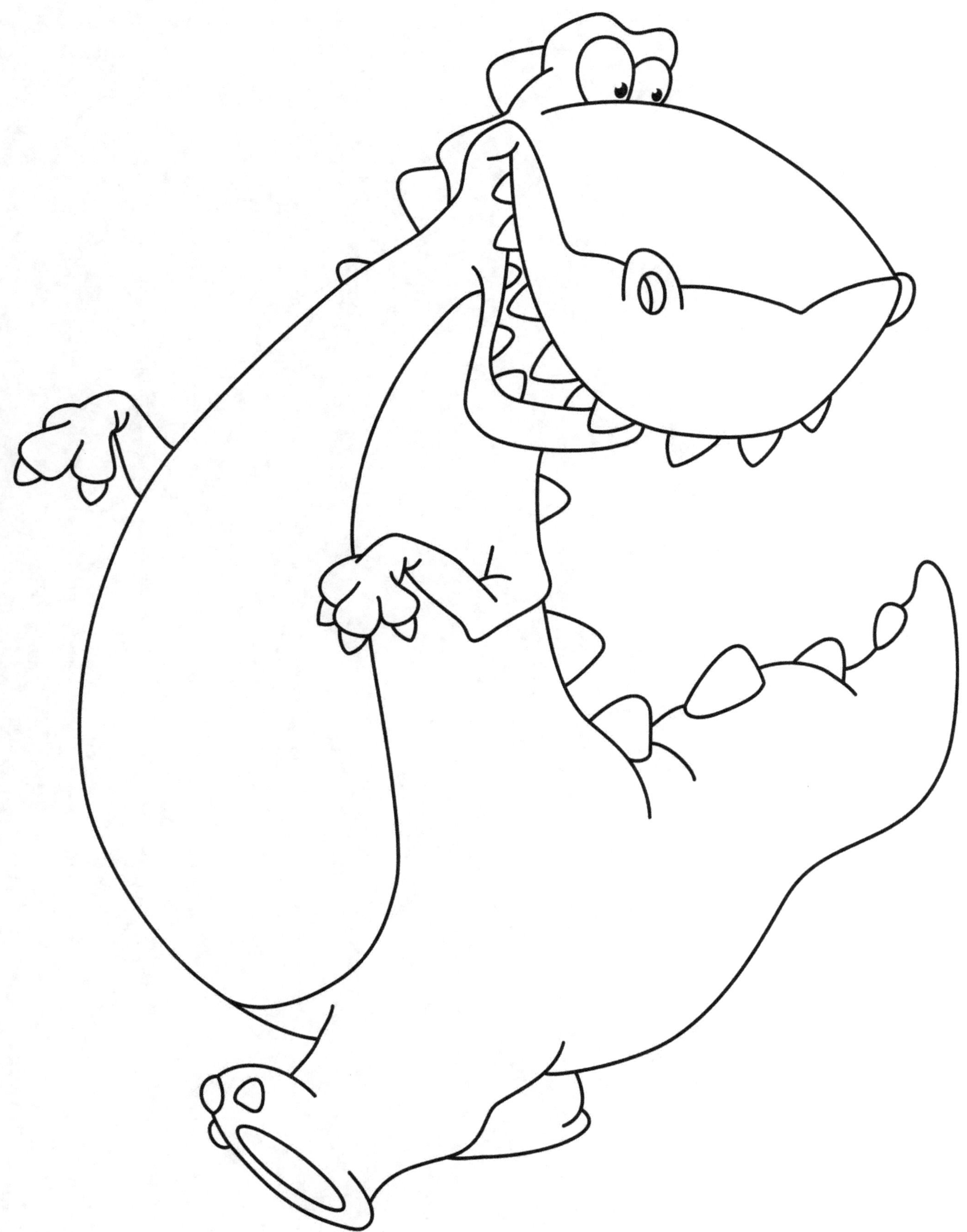

www.ingramcontent.com/pod-product-compliance
Lightning Source LLC
Chambersburg PA
CBHW080314030726
47593CB00009B/2740